══ 168 ══
MORE BUSINESSES
ANYONE CAN START
AND MAKE A LOT OF
MONEY

―――――――― 2ND EDITION ――――――――

BANTAM BUSINESS BOOKS

Entrepreneur®

MAGAZINE'S

168

MORE BUSINESSES
ANYONE CAN START
AND MAKE A LOT OF
MONEY

2ND EDITION

THE EDITORS OF

Entrepreneur®

BANTAM BOOKS

NEW YORK · TORONTO · LONDON · SYDNEY · AUCKLAND

168 MORE BUSINESSES ANYONE CAN START AND MAKE A LOT OF
MONEY
A Bantam Book / September 1984
Revised edition / April 1991

Library of Congress Cataloging-in-Publication Data

168 more businesses anyone can start and make a lot of money / the
editors of Entrepreneur. — Rev. ed.
    p.   cm.
  ISBN 0-553-35238-5
  1. New business enterprises.   2. Success in business.   3. Small
business.   I. Entrepreneur (Santa Monica, Calif.)   II. Title: One
hundred sixty-eight more businesses anyone can start and make a lot
of money.
HD62.5.A14   1991
658.1'141—dc20
                                                            90-38908
                                                            CIP

Published simultaneously in the United States and Canada

Bantam Books are published by Bantam Books, a division of Bantam
Doubleday Dell Publishing Group, Inc. Its trademark, consisting of
the words "Bantam Books" and the portrayal of a rooster, is Regis-
tered in U.S. Patent and Trademark Office and in other countries.
Marca Registrada. Bantam Books, 666 Fifth Avenue, New York, New
York 10103.

CONTENTS

1
FOOD

2
PERSONAL SERVICES

3
BUSINESS SERVICES

4

MISCELLANEOUS SERVICES

5

COMPUTER BUSINESSES

6

RETAIL

7

SPORTS AND ENTERTAINMENT

8
AUTOMOTIVE BUSINESSES

9
OUT OF THE ORDINARY

ACKNOWLEDGMENTS

Thousands and thousands of hours of research have gone into creating this book. For much of it, we are indebted to the staff, past and present, of *Entrepreneur*® magazine. Particular thanks go to Maria Anton, Christine Forbes, Charles Fuller, Frances Huffman, Maria Johnson, Erika Kotite, Kevin McLaughlin, Frank Mixson, and Gayle Sato.

We'd also like to express our gratitude to Barbara Alpert of Bantam, a wonderful editor, who had the vision to bring these books to life.

Rieva Lesonsky, Editor
Entrepreneur® magazine

INTRODUCTION

The 1990s—there has never been a better time to start and operate your own business. Even the United States Congress recognizes the entrepreneurial revolution currently under-way in America and has declared the 1990s to be "The Dec-ade of the Entrepreneur."

Every year, over one million Americans join this entrepre-neurial revolution. In fact, business ownership has become one of the nation's biggest status symbols. Why? Some say they're fed up working hard to put money in someone else's pocket. Many believe they're underpaid and unappreciated for what they do. Others seek the satisfaction that only "charting your own course" brings. Whatever the reason, these entrepreneurial "recruits" have signed into an army over 20 million strong and growing.

Wouldn't you like to be one of them? Well, you can be. It's not as difficult or as frightening as you may think. At *Entre-preneur*® magazine, we know that business ownership serves as a great equalizer. There is no discrimination against a great new product or a much needed service. There are no "glass ceilings" to bump your head against. It doesn't matter what race, religion, or sex you are. Age is of no impor-tance. Over the 17 years we've been in business, we've seen successful businesses started by 16-year-olds, as well as those over 60.

You're probably wondering, if entrepreneurship is so great, why aren't there more entrepreneurs? What keeps so many from business ownership? Fear! People are afraid they don't have enough money to start a business. Or they can't think of a good business idea. Or they mistakenly think that their job offers them security, while entrepreneurship is too risky.

But taking the risk is essential to receiving the rewards. Remember (at the risk of sounding like a high school coach), if you don't swing the bat, you'll never get a hit.

We're not saying that starting your own business is easy. It's not! But almost every entrepreneur we've ever met says the hard work that business start-up entails is worth it. Nothing, they say, equals the satisfaction and rewards (both financially and psychologically) of business ownership.

And, believe it or not, you don't need a lot of money to get started. Many of today's most successful entrepreneurs started their now-giant corporations out of their homes (or garages) on a very limited budget.

What about the idea? That's probably the easiest part. You don't necessarily have to reinvent the wheel. There are thousands of great ideas out there waiting for you to run with them. You don't have to be the first at anything to succeed. McDonald's was not the first hamburger joint. And the Colonel certainly did not invent fried chicken.

What you do need to do is be alert. Look around your community. What's lacking? Is someone doing something you could do better? Or quicker? Or cheaper? Chances are if there's a product or service you're personally seeking, but can't find, others in your area want it, too. And they'd be willing to pay for it. Question your friends, neighbors, and relatives. Find the common thread.

Simply reading this book may be the spark you've been looking for. It is just one in a series from the editors of *Entrepreneur®* magazine. In it (and the others) you'll find hundreds of ideas for businesses you can start NOW!

Most important, you need to get started. A successful business owner once told me, "The biggest obstacle to business success is the four words, 'I think I'll wait.'" Don't let this happen to you. If you dream of someday owning your own business, pursue it. Sure, you're going to encounter obstacles and setbacks along the way. But determination and persistence pay off. You can turn your dreams into reality.

Only one thing can hold you back: not getting started. Remember these words, written by Goethe, an 18th-century poet, "Whatever you can do or dream, begin it. Boldness has genius, power and magic in it. Begin it now!"

Rieva Lesonsky, Editor
Entrepreneur® magazine

168

MORE BUSINESSES ANYONE CAN START AND MAKE A LOT OF MONEY

2ND EDITION

FOED

GOURMET TO GO

Ah, the 1990s. Your commute takes 45 minutes—each way. You work fifty hours a week meeting unreasonable deadlines, bickering with your boss, and tinkering with an un-cooperative computer. You dash to the day-care center to pick up the kids on time. Then you fetch the dry cleaning, run by the drugstore, take your shoes in for repair, and pick up your mother-in-law's birthday present. Wouldn't it be wonderful if a good, hot meal were waiting for you when you got home?

Thanks to a new breed of take-out, a good, hot meal is just a phone call away for thousands of working Americans. Twenty years ago, fast food was innovation enough. Once in a while, the family could run out and get a burger and fries. But today, people are eating out more than ever. And the burger and fries that was good enough once a month does not look as good five times a week.

Enter the gourmet take-out. These operations range from specially outfitted catering trucks to storefronts and delivery services. They all have one thing in common: good food that you can eat in the comfort of your own home. Entrées include anything from chicken veronique to vegetarian lasagna, prime rib to cioppino. At some take-outs, food is dished up hot. At others, entrées are frozen and reheated at home.

There is room in this business for individual style. The only constants are convenience and a love for food. Look for a relatively upscale location with plenty of working professionals and older people who don't like to cook.

COFFEE AND TEA SHOP

High Net Profit Before Taxes:	$90,000
Average Net Profit Before Taxes:	$65,000
Minimum Start-up:	$40,000
Average Start-up:	$60,000

A good cup of coffee isn't what it used to be—it's better. Today, savvy consumers discuss the richness of the roast, the acidity of the brew, the subtle shadings of Costa Rican, Jamaican, and Celebesian blends. For decaf drinkers, the question of process is important (only water-process will do). Coffee consumers can be as fussy as wine connoisseurs, and just about as willing to spend.

Tea drinkers are equally enthusiastic. Many hard-line coffee drinkers have switched to tea in recent years, and not all of them are happy with a basic box of Lipton's. Imported Darjeeling, jasmine, and chamomile are just a few favored choices. This in addition to teapots, tea balls, spoon infusers, coffeemakers, cold-water toddies, filters, mugs, jugs, and espresso makers. Done properly, a gourmet coffee and tea store can offer a lot more than something hot to drink.

Check Out Your Local Market

The next time you're grocery shopping, check out the coffee and tea aisle. Between the Nestea and the Maxwell House, you're likely to find some rather upscale offerings. Some stores have even installed gourmet coffee centers, complete with in-store grinders.

Does this spell trouble for specialty coffee and tea retailers in your area? Not necessarily. True-blue gourmets turn up their noses at the grocery-store goods. And the mere fact that the mass market has picked up on this trend indicates how far-reaching it is. The real challenge for gourmet retailers is staying ahead of the competition with exceptional quality and service.

Steeped in Profits

One 250-square-foot family-owned shop we found is pulling in more than $250,000 annually in coffee alone. Another outfit that started as a local coffee service has grown into a chain that grosses an average of $300,000 per store.

In most markets, an owner-operator willing to learn about the distinctive characteristics of coffees and teas from around the world can look at an annual pretax net of 20 percent based on a minimum investment of $30,000. Profit margins are high, and repeat customers are virtually guaranteed from the day you open your shop.

The Perfect Brew

Operations with superhigh profits all had three things in common: top-quality gourmet coffee beans and teas, a prime location with plenty of foot traffic, and a friendly but upscale atmosphere.

Typical gourmet coffee and tea buyers are well-educated, from 25 to 45 years old. About 75 percent are women. More than a third may have incomes of $40,000 or more, with some 20 percent in the $30,000 to $40,000 bracket.

An understanding of ethnic or regional preferences in your market will help. Chicory coffee is familiar in the South, while in urbanized areas there will be a bigger interest in espresso, spiced blends, and imported tea. A Cuban or Spanish roast is more likely to appeal to the Miami market than to shoppers in Milwaukee.

Finding the Right Space

Locate your shop where you can draw plenty of the right kind of foot traffic. Remember that your market is upscale.

The area you serve can have as few as 30,000 residents if income averages above $20,000.

Customers should know at a glance what kind of shop you have. Your best bet is a storefront in a stylish strip shopping center or busy shopping district. Find out what kinds of customers frequent the area and get an idea of traffic flow by spending a couple of days people-watching. If there is a good volume of foot traffic, you can lure shoppers in by offering an inexpensive cup of gourmet coffee or tea to go. Once shoppers are hooked on your brew, they'll return to buy larger stashes for home use.

Malls are also good locations, though high rents and heavy front-end expenses make this a more costly alternative. Converting a new mall space into a coffee store can run up to $50,000, or from $15,000 to $20,000 in an existing site that's been vacated.

You can set up a profitable store in 600 square feet of space. One very profitable operation in only 240 square feet offers thirty-four coffees and forty teas and is grossing six figures annually. With careful planning, you can stock and display a wide variety of coffees, teas, spices, and coffee- and tea-making accessories in a limited space.

═══════════════════BRIGHT IDEA═══════════════════

SHAVED ICE

First there was ice cream. Then there was frozen yogurt. What's next? Could it be shaved ice? Iona Bucklew, president of Mountain Snow Franchise Operations Inc., a Morgantown, West Virginia-based shaved-ice franchise, certainly thinks so. "I feel that shaved ice is going to be as popular as frozen yogurt," she says. "It has no fat, no cholesterol, and the flavors are super."

Shaved ice—not to be confused with snow cones—is a fairly new concept in the United States—or at least on the mainland. Actually, Hawaiians have been enjoying the low-calorie dessert for years. The snowlike ice, shaved from an ice block as it rotates on a shaving machine, is served in a bowl with a choice of flavored toppings. And its popularity is growing daily.

Shaved-ice vendors operate their businesses from both permanent restaurant locations and mobile ones—including trucks, and carts. The start-up cost for a shaved-ice business ranges from $1,000 to $18,000, and the product is typically sold at prices competitive with those charged for ice cream and frozen yogurt. In addition to shaved ice, vendors often supplement their income—and their customers' palates— with other items like deli sandwiches or muffins.

===================== BRIGHT IDEA =====================

ALL IN GOOD TASTE

"People were afraid to eat artichokes," says Melissa Russell, co-owner of In-Store Demos Inc., in Los Angeles. Yet after the California Artichoke Board signed a contract with Russell and partner Nina Segovia allowing them to place trained demonstrators in grocery stores, a Phoenix, Arizona grocery store sold more than 900 artichokes in one day.

"Our demonstrators showed shoppers how to cook artichokes for dinner or appetizers and how to eat the artichokes politely. We made people aware that this cooked vegetable has only 25 calories," says Russell.

In-Store Demos has done similar work for other food companies. Although giving out free samples was common in the 1950s, it wasn't until the late 1980s that the demonstration of samples experienced a resurgence. The high price of media time and space has encouraged food companies to move away from traditional advertising to the more personal samplings and demonstrations.

Industry experts argue that, dollar for dollar, sampling is more economical than many other kinds of advertising. Consumers can't resist sampling (and hopefully purchasing) a product when a sharp, personable demonstrator touts the benefits of the item. In the end, both the consumer and the food producer benefit.

Sampling is precisely the kind of service for which food

manufacturers contract out. For a comparatively modest fee, a food company can avoid the hassles of hiring and training demonstrators, buying basic equipment and supplies, negotiating with supermarkets, and tracking the results. On the other hand, a food sampling company with an existing pool of qualified workers, supermarket contacts, and set-ups can produce continual profits.

Russell and Segovia hire college students and others for part-time demonstrator positions. The partners provide training sessions for their employees and pay them up to $9 per hour to promote everything from ice cream to rum cake. Their revenues: $200,000 their first year in business, and $300,000 their second.

HERB FARMING

High Net Profit Before Taxes:	$99,800
Average Net Profit Before Taxes:	$45,900
Minimum Start-up:	$3,740
Average Start-up:	$30,000

A good herb used to be hard to find. These days, thanks to a growing herb farming industry, that isn't so. In recent years, Americans have discovered the value of a good herb—and for more than just spicing up their favorite foods. While culinary herbs represent a large market for herb farmers, consumers are also buying herbs for landscaping, crafts, cosmetics, and health.

Back on the Farm

Believe it or not, you can start a part-time herb farming business in the big city. As long as you have access to a good-sized plot of land, you can cultivate hardy herbs and sell them to local restaurants and grocery stores. A small garden won't reap a huge profit, but you can tend it on your off-hours and bring in additional cash. And if you enjoy gardening anyway, you can consider herb farming a kind of paid leisure.

With even a relatively small space, however, you can turn a tidy profit. Herbs command premium prices, so even a few well-cultivated acres can bring in good money. Farmers who tend more traditional crops sometimes devote a small parcel of land to herbs, but you don't have to live on a farm to be an herb farmer. If you're especially resourceful, you can grow a few acres worth of crops in odd spaces—renting vacant lots, backyards, rooftops, greenhouses, and so on.

What Will Your Garden Grow?

The key to herb farming is knowing what the market wants. Would-be herbalists who don't know fennel from fenugreek have a lot to learn. Established herb farmers suggest reading up on herbs and gardening before starting the business, and also checking local markets to see what's in demand.

Restaurants, for example, may want fresh herbs like basil, rosemary, thyme, and dill, as well as exotic vegetables like arugula, radicchio, and mache. Herbal tea companies may be more partial to chamomile, mint, lemon grass, and rose hips, while naturopaths, who use herbs for medicinal purposes, have other interests entirely.

Your success in this business hinges on the desirability of the crops you grow. Research the local—and national—markets available to you. Once you've determined who is likely to buy from you, you can determine which herbs to grow.

Show Your Green Thumb

Successful herb farmers agree that the market for these crops is large and growing. But that doesn't make this a foolproof business. Like any farming, herb farming is subject to the whims of nature—not to mention the ravages of ignorance. A green thumb is not only an advantage in this business, it's a virtual must. Learning everything you can about irrigation systems, soil preparation, pest control, and proper harvesting is just good sense.

Profitable as it is, herb farming is not the business for everyone. However, those who have a knack for growing things and a disdain for modern urbanity find it a rewarding way to make a living. Few other modern-day professions allow you to spend the day outdoors among fragrant plants. Perhaps it's not life in the fast lane, but for many independent herb farmers, that's just the point.

══════════════ BRIGHT IDEA ══════════════

TERIYAKI BOWLS

You don't have to be Japanese to appreciate the flavor of teriyaki beef and chicken. Many mainstream restaurants have added teriyaki to their menus—and now, so have new fast-food joints that serve nothing but this popular item.

Teriyaki bowls are a simple combination of steamed rice and grilled chicken or beef brushed with teriyaki sauce. By using lean beef and skinless chicken, you can call your fare healthful as well as inexpensive and fast. Inventory requirements are minimal—just rice, meat, and teriyaki sauce (which you can buy premade or make yourself with a few simple ingredients).

Who buys fast-food teriyaki? The same folks who eat pizza and hamburgers for lunch or dinner every day. As in any other fast-food operation, convenience and foot traffic are the hallmarks of a good location. One operation we spotted works from a "food court," surrounded by pizza, fish and chips, hamburger, and sandwich shops, and is still averaging 800 bowls per day. Some shops operate in as little as 300 square feet. An 800-square-foot location will give you plenty of food-preparation space and allow customers a place to sit.

Play up the ethnic flavor of your business: Hang Japanese prints on the walls and have employees sport matching hapi coats (short versions of kimonos). Take a tip from the Japanese, though—don't offer chopsticks. According to similar operations in Japan, chopsticks will slow down the eating time of your patrons.

CATERING SERVICE

High Net Profit Before Taxes:	$150,000-plus
Average Net Profit Before Taxes:	$85,000
Minimum Start-up:	$62,000
Average Start-up:	$85,000

Catering may be a low-investment opportunity, but it isn't small potatoes. According to the National Caterers Association, caterers made close to $5 billion in 1987.

Catering has become big business, not just for hotels and restaurants, but for entrepreneurs as well. "It's one of the few things an independent can get into with either a small or large investment," says Tony Rubino, a food and beverage consultant and president of the National Caterers Association. "Of the 40,000 caterers in the country, only about one-third gross less than $100,000 a year."

Even if you're just a weekend caterer, the profits can be high. Catering even one party of 100 people may gross as much as $3,000. So if you cater four events a month, that's $144,000 a year.

What's Your Specialty?

A catering business can specialize in anything from "appetizers only" to organizing an entire event, including invitations, flowers, food, beverages, entertainment, and limousine service, all in one package. The services you offer depend mainly on where you live. For instance, in large cities, corporate catering is probably the most lucrative. Caterers who specialize in corporate luncheons and cocktail parties are in high demand. For harried executives, holding a meeting or even a client luncheon in the office conference room is more relaxing and productive than fighting crowds on the sidewalk and in restaurants.

Then of course there are weddings—which take place in towns of every size. Nearly every wedding reception is handled by a caterer who is either on-premise (i.e., part of the hotel, restaurant, or hall staff) or off-premise (works from the client's location). The caterers may provide anything from

simple cold cuts and punch to an elaborate five-course meal,
complete with champagne, intermezzo, and finger bowls.
Often, catering a wedding means more than bringing food—
decorations, music, and wedding favors may also be part of
the caterer's contract.

Corporate events and weddings are two common specialties, but they are by no means the only ones. Birthdays,
anniversaries, and even funerals require catering services on
a regular basis. One Florida entrepreneur specializes in company picnics. In addition to food, he provides entertainment
and a carnival dunk tank.

Starting from Scratch

There are hundreds of ways to break into the catering
business. Many entrepreneurs start small from home, but
local health regulations may prohibit you from doing this. If
home cooking is prohibited in your area, consider renting a
health-licensed church kitchen or other alternative facility.
One Kansas entrepreneur rented bakery space from a grocery
store for a year—just long enough to establish the business
and find her own commercial location.

Commercial kitchens are used specifically to prepare food
for the public, which means they must be inspected and
approved by the local health department. Many caterers rent
commercial kitchens (which don't cost as much as you might
think) for the large ovens and refrigerators. Many churches,
halls, and clubs also have kitchens which they will rent to
aspiring caterers at reasonable rates. "These places are fully
equipped, health-inspected facilities," says Rubino. "This
saves you from putting together a commissary, paying rent,
and buying equipment. A caterer can essentially start with
just a telephone. Getting started doesn't have to cost a lot of
money."

Business Sense

Being a good caterer means knowing how to cook and put
together a menu, but it also means knowing how to run a
business. One important factor is marketing. Most caterers
get plenty of business through referrals, but in order to grow,

caterers must always be on the lookout for new clients and must promote their services through publicity and advertising. This may be as simple as advertising in the Yellow Pages, or volunteering services for a charitable fund-raiser.

Having a good mix of big parties and small parties is important, too. Big parties gross more. For example, a wedding reception for 200 people at $20 a head will gross $4,000. It would take 10 parties of 20 people to equal that sum, and needless to say, it would involve many more hours of work. It might be hard to turn down any job, no matter how small, but being selective about your clients may be more profitable in the long run.

Getting—and keeping—good suppliers, both for food and nonfood items, can significantly increase the caterer's bottom line. The local supermarket may be perfectly satisfactory for most parties. In fact, it may be more reasonable than other suppliers in certain cases. You can use the supermarket for smaller parties, and also maintain a list of quality meat, produce, and seafood suppliers in your area. Most wholesale grocers offer delivery, and since every minute counts when you're preparing for a large party, free delivery translates into added profit.

With more and more people, especially women, joining the work force, planning a party or even a family dinner is becoming a luxury few people can afford. It also means that the catering industry will continue to grow. And for aspiring cooks with a flair for partying, that means tasty profits—Bon appetit!

========= BRIGHT IDEA =========

THE FLYING BURRITO

Moving, even if it's just across town, can make anyone feel homesick. But real transplants miss more than just their old friends; the flavor of their local cuisine is often what they yearn for most. New Englanders who move west long for the fresh clam chowder and seafood that can't be found in other parts of the country. For Southwesterners who move east, it's the lack of authentic Mexican food that dampens their spirits.

Coming to their rescue is Burrito Express, a unique service created by a pair of native Mexicans, Vic and Lila Cuadra, to satisfy homesick palates. The couple ship burritos from their Pasadena, California, restaurant to Mexican food connoisseurs from coast to coast. "When I heard that the thing ex-Californians miss most is Mexican food, I decided to help," says Vic.

The restaurateur makes his burritos fresh, quick-freezes them, and then sends them overnight in a specially designed six-pack. They arrive frozen the next morning, and all the recipient has to do is pop them into the microwave. They're worth the effort. These aren't wimpy supermarket burritos. The hefty combo burritos weigh in at about 10 ounces and come in chicken, beef, or pork—mild for gringos, spicy for the brave.

For now, Burrito Express customers are locals who ship the spicy fare to friends and relatives who have moved away. Most of the six-packs, which sell for $31.25 (delivery included), find their way to areas where Mexican food is scarce.

While the restaurant business still accounts for the majority of revenues at Burrito Express, sales of the overnight burritos have increased from 1 percent to 10 percent of the company's revenues in just one year. As the flying burritos gain in popularity, you can't help but wonder what will be next. Are you ready for flying chowder?

CANDY STORE

High Net Profit Before Taxes:	$100,000
Average Net Profit Before Taxes:	$40,000
Minimum Start-up:	$23,000
Average Start-up:	$50,000

If your idea of a fabulous job is being up to your elbows in fudge, a candy store could be the business for you. Though there's nothing new about the candy business, there are plenty of new ideas being tried. Say good-bye to plain old peppermint sticks and low-key lollipops. Today's candy is as irresistible to adults as it is to kids. And better still, it's more lucrative.

Grown-up Tastes

For dyed-in-the-wool sweet tooths, candy is pretty irresistible in any form. But suppose you visited a shop where employees made fudge right before your eyes? Could you resist trying a small bag—or buying a box for friends? What if the shop sold nothing but chocolate: chocolate sculptures, chocolate fudge sauce, roasted almonds dipped in chocolate and cocoa? Wouldn't you be tempted to buy just a little something?

Of course you would. When you were a child, it probably seemed that candy stores knew exactly how to pull your strings. Just walking through the doors was a treat. Now you're grown up—and so is the candy business. The bait has changed—now it's more likely to be ultra-rich chocolates and homemade caramels than gumballs and jawbreakers—but the effect is identical. The most jaded of us get wide-eyed at the sight of candy.

Sour Economy, Sweet Tooth

Perhaps that's why candy is one of the few items on the open market that actually sells better when the economy turns sour. A cheap sweet does wonders for the psyche. And the candy business can do wonders for you.

You can enter this industry in many ways. Test your recipes by selling candy at roadside stands and fairs. Or rent a commercial kitchen and sell your packaged goods to gift shops and boutiques. One operator we found does this on a part-time basis and grosses more than $50,000 annually.

When you're ready to set up shop, your space doesn't have to be fancy (though it should meet health department codes). We found successful operations in converted churches, filling stations, garages, houses, even on a converted fishing boat.

A Look at the Market

America's collective sweet tooth is divided into four main target areas:

• The youth market (ages 6 to 18) is attracted to candy bars, confections, and heavy sweets such as caramels, nougats, and chocolate.

• The young adult market (ages 18 to 35) is primarily interested in high quality and variety: upscale chocolate confections (truffles, twigs, nuts), exotic candies, and candy gimmicks.

• The older adult market (35 and over) prefers more basic candies—chocolates, caramels, and so on.

• Health fanatics, a new market in the candy business, are looking for candy that has a sweet taste and nutritional value. Low-sugar (or no-sugar) varieties are also popular.

The young adult and older adult markets usually have more discretionary income and are willing to pay more for quality. Statistics show that 51 percent of all candy sold, including chocolate, is now consumed by adults. Clearly, this is where the action is.

Income levels are also important in determining what kind of candy your customer will buy. Blue-collar areas favor basic candy like fudge, brittle, and caramel. More affluent areas will respond to unusual items—chocolate-dipped fruit, chocolate sculptures, and so on.

Women and children appear to make up about 70 percent of candy customers. Adult males who buy candy are often looking for gifts.

What's in Your Own Backyard?

What kind of community do you need to support a profitable candy store? A population of 200,000 is a good median base. The community should have a good mix of industries and services and a relatively high standard of living. Key locations are densely populated with families—areas with condominiums, apartments, and other multifamily dwellings.

Since buying candy is an impulse act, the more foot traffic and browsers you have, the better your chance for high profits. There are candy stores in every conceivable location: strip shopping centers, shopping malls, single-site locations, converted churches, circus wagons, old train cars, boats—any place that attracts crowds on a continuous basis.

If you're especially frugal, you can start a candy store for less than $25,000, though average investments range around $50,000 to $60,000. You can make pretax profits of $40,000 to $100,000 a year with smart planning, hard work, and the right selection of products.

LUNCH DELIVERY

Busy employees can't always go to lunch. So in many buildings, lunch comes to them. Lunch delivery services provide a convenient brown-bag alternative to thousands of hungry office workers—and a low-cost opportunity to many new business owners.

Successful operations we investigated started out as catering companies. During the week, when the catering business was slow, they would fill coolers with simple sandwiches, salads, and desserts and wheel them around to local office buildings. For one such company, lunch delivery became so lucrative that the owner got out of catering altogether.

You don't have to be a caterer to get into this business, however. All you need is a health-licensed kitchen to prepare food and portable coolers to deliver it. Can't cook? Enlist the help of a local restaurant or deli. Offer to buy sandwiches, salads, and microwaveable entrées from them at discounted prices. They'll increase their volume and gain valuable exposure; you won't have to rent a kitchen or do any cooking.

Standards are surprisingly high in the lunch-delivery business, particularly in areas with competition between companies. You don't have to offer fancy fare, but you should stress quality, variety, and value if you hope to attract regular customers. Reliability is another important factor. Be friendly, be prompt, but most of all, be there every day. If customers can depend on you for wholesome, fast, inexpensive food, your business will be a continuing success.

DINER

High Net Profit Before Taxes:	$937,000
Average Net Profit Before Taxes:	$590,000
Minimum Start-up:	$212,000
Average Start-up:	$370,000

The foodies of America have come to a startling realization: Man cannot live by duck sausage and baby vegetables alone. In fact, most of us would really rather have meatloaf.

Meatloaf? Yes, and burgers, fries, pie, and milkshakes. Forget everything you've read about the evils of cholesterol. Good old American cooking tastes great—especially in the uniquely American ambience of the good old five-and-dime diner. A few years back, people started rediscovering the appeal of chrome, leatherette, jukeboxes, and chicken-fried steak. And while diners aren't the news they were when Ed Debevics first sprang onto the scene, they are still attracting a loyal and nostalgic following.

A Look Back

Today's diners sell more than meat and potatoes—they also dish up a healthy serving of nostalgia. In a world plagued by drugs, crime, pollution, stress, heart disease, and a host of other downers, it's a comfort to be served simple fare by a gum-cracking waitress while listening to Buddy Holly. But don't think the clientele at America's diners is limited to folks who remember the fifties and sixties. On the contrary, young adults and teens are avid diner customers.

Diners are purely American. They've been around since 1872, when a Providence, Rhode Island entrepreneur named Walter Scott opened a beanery on wheels to serve drivers of horse-drawn express trucks. From that tiny beanery, the diner evolved into large manufactured wagons set up so people could eat inside them, and most were placed on rented plots of land to better serve the public. Throughout the thirties, forties, and fifties, these dining cars or "diners" flourished, until the emergence of drive-in and fast-food restaurants.

It wasn't just the unique design that brought in customers; it was also the food. Thanks to the original diners, chili, hot dogs, and blue-plate specials have found a permanent place in the American palate. This isn't food you have to get used to—no marinated jicama, no sautéed chayote. Perhaps it isn't gourmet fare, but it is familiar.

Authenticity Plus

Re-creating a real diner can be a difficult and painstaking process. For real nostalgia buffs, authenticity is a must. Many diner owners have located old dining cars and restored them to their old glory with fabulous results. But this kind of authenticity is optional. Many a successful diner has been established in a modern location with the right decor and paraphernalia.

Sticking to old diner fare is optional, too. Most diners still feature standards like meatloaf, mashed potatoes, burgers, and fries. But many have added updated favorites: chicken sandwiches, quiche, salads, and omelets. Some put a twist on the old ways—Cajun-spiced meatloaf, gourmet burgers, fresh steamed vegetables in the place of canned. Customers seem less concerned with rigid authenticity than good eats.

Yet while authenticity isn't essential, a sense of nostalgia is. To create a real diner, you will need certain props. A jukebox is a must—preferably stocked with hits from the forties or fifties. Old movie posters, old-fashioned menu signs, and fun uniforms all make for the right atmosphere. And don't be afraid to go overboard. Tacking old 45s up on the wall or using poodle skirts for decorations isn't out of line if the effect is witty and different.

Beyond the Image

When diners first started gaining in popularity, the food industry wondered how long the fad would last. And indeed, some new diners have gone the way of the old. Today, diners aren't guaranteed hits. Like any other restaurant, they require sound management, good promotion, a competent staff, and excellent food to endure. But for entrepreneurs with imagination, style, and an eye toward the past, few businesses offer as much down-home charm.

================== BRIGHT IDEA ==================

CHOCOLATE MANIA

Chocolate is a $4.8-billion industry in America, and we aren't done bingeing yet. Many of life's luxuries are becoming too expensive to justify: $50,000 autos and $2,000 suits are simply out of the question for most of us. But even an expensive piece of chocolate weighs in at under $2—and it can make you feel like a million.

What's hot in chocolate? These days, upscale items are selling best. Indulgence is the word of the day, and chocolate products that offer pure ingredients and intense flavors are among the most popular. Additionally, single-servings are selling well. Apparently, controlled portions equal controlled guilt. Of course, that doesn't rule out large-ticket items like wedding cakes, gift baskets, and wholesale sales. These also represent a huge and hungry market.

Within these parameters, however, almost anything goes. From basics like brownies, cookies, cakes, and candies to chocolate sculptures, chocolate-dipped potato chips, bottled chocolate sauce, chocolate lace, chocolate bark, chocolate pasta, ice cream, cheesecake, and fruit, nothing seems too outrageous for America's chocolate lovers. And don't forget auxiliary businesses like equipment manufacturing, marketing, packaging, distributing, and so on. Now that America's chocoholics have come out of the closet, almost anything is possible.

MEXICAN RESTAURANT

High Net Profit Before Taxes:	$76,000-plus
Average Net Profit Before Taxes:	$50,000
Minimum Start-up:	$55,000
Average Start-up:	$100,000

Variety is the spice of life—and spice is the secret of success in this fast-growing segment of the restaurant industry. The growth rate for Mexican restaurants is currently about 11 percent per year, jumping from $2.5 billion in 1986 to $2.8 billion in 1987, according to *Restaurant Business* magazine. And since many parts of the country are just catching on to Mexican cuisine, now is the time to throw your sombrero into the ring.

Hot Profits

Large chain outlets can cost as much as $1.5 million to start, but you don't have to spend anywhere near that much to break into this business. Your investment will vary with your local market, but $55,000 is not unthinkable with the proper planning.

Better still, profit potential in a Mexican restaurant is unusually high. In typical restaurants and fast-food outlets, food costs run from 33 to 45 percent. In this business they're closer to 28 or 30 percent. Consumers also get a good deal, spending an average of $3 to $7 per meal.

At these prices, weekly gross volumes in food alone can average from $10,000 to $25,000. With beverage sales, this can work out to a minimum of $60,000 per month. Despite overhead, it's still possible to bring a solid 25 to 30 percent to the bottom line—far above the industry average for food-service establishments.

Strike While the Salsa Is Hot

The popularity of Mexican food has not escaped the notice of franchisors (some might even credit them with the trend). Mexican fast-food outlets like Taco Bell have spread across the country, making Mexican food far less exotic than it once was.

But you don't have to go head-to-head with major chains to compete. Franchising is not the whole story in this business. In order to appeal to the broadest customer base, franchise operations have relatively mild sauces and garnishes. As a result, despite heavy promotions, they can lose customers with more adventurous palates. Also, fast food can't do justice to the wide range of dishes that comprise Mexican cooking. A full-service restaurant can.

Now that America's appetite for Mexican food has been whetted, it's time for a more innovative approach. With menu pizzazz and a little street-smart marketing, an independent can set standards of cuisine, service, and value that the average chain can't touch.

Low Price, High Value

Mexican restaurants offer diners an alternative to the usual steak, pasta, and sushi. Better still, most Mexican restaurants are relatively inexpensive, making them a good value as well as a novelty.

Mexican food, unlike most types of ethnic foods, appeals to both "light" and "heavy" eaters. Many Mexican dishes are light in character, a fact that is just beginning to be realized by the market. Also, many Mexican dishes are vegetarian. Some 25 percent of those who eat Mexican dishes prefer them meatless. This contributes to the lightness of many Mexican meals and widens their appeal.

A Choice of Set-ups

Three basic Mexican restaurant concepts dominate the industry. One is the fast-food operation offering a limited menu, counter service, and a seating capacity of less than fifty—if there are seats at all. The second popular option is a full-service restaurant, with or without a bar, seating between sixty and 100 people. The third option, which has become increasingly popular around the country, combines the limited- or full-service restaurant with take-out, boosting profits by 25 to 50 percent in some areas.

Whichever concept you choose, it's important to emphasize the freshness and quality of your product. In most areas,
chains are already providing fast, cheap, and generally bland
Mexican food. While some markets are decidedly unreceptive
to spicy foods, many consumers are willing to try recipes
with a little heat if they reflect authentic flavors. Assess your
market carefully, remembering that your best bet isn't to
duplicate the fast-food chains, but to take advantage of the
niches they've opened.

=============== BRIGHT IDEA ===============

MAKE MINE BLACK

Looking to invent the next big food fad? Think black. *The
New York Times* reports that black food is the latest twist in
culinary delights. The color can add a richer flavor to food, as
well as giving a meal a certain aesthetic appeal. These dark
delights include black rice, black olives, black mushrooms,
black seaweed, black pasta, and black beans.

A brand of black popcorn has even been introduced to
grocery stores nationwide by St. Francisville, Illinois-based
Black Jewell Popcorn, Inc. Black Jewell popcorn was developed for its unique, sweeter flavor, its lack of hulls, and its
tender, crunchy texture. And the company points out that
black, not white, is the natural color of popcorn anyhow.

PASTA RESTAURANT

High Net Profit Before Taxes:	$100,000-plus
Average Net Profit Before Taxes:	$65,000
Minimum Start-up:	$95,000
Average Start-up:	$133,000

Please, don't call it spaghetti. Today's pasta comes in an
assortment of shapes and sizes, from flat farfalle to tubular
penne. There are more kinds of sauce than you can name on
a page: roasted garlic and broccoli, Gorgonzola and cream,

sausage and peppers, white-wine clam, and—of course—
good old marinara. With so much to choose from, it's no
wonder American consumers never seem to get tired of
pasta. And with noodles, there's none of the fear and loathing
that raw fish, alligator steaks, and other bizarre ethnic foods
tend to inspire.

But that's not the only good news for aspiring food entrepreneurs. A plate of pasta can cost as little as 59 cents to
make, and can sell for upwards of $3.00. The most suc-
cessful shops we talked to were grossing from $200,000 to
$1.8 million annually with basic operations that can be du-
plicated in virtually any city.

The Perfect Fast Food?

Pasta is ideally suited to an upscale fast-food operation.
Because your cost of production is so low, you can offer good,
hearty pasta meals—complete with soft drink and garlic
bread—for as little as $3.00. Additional profits from beer and
wine sales are also a possibility. Use a little culinary creativity, invest in an attractive decor, and you could become the
hottest fast food on the block.

Remember that pasta is healthy as well as delicious. With
more and more people watching their diets, you should have
no trouble luring customers away from the usual greasy
burgers and fries. And since many pasta recipes don't call for
meat, you can cater to the vegetarian market successfully.

Lunch represents the busiest meal for most fast-food
pasta operations. Be on the alert for locations with heavy
lunchtime foot traffic. An urban high-rise shopping and
business district is ideal. Having a college campus nearby is
an added plus. You might also consider locating in a large
shopping mall. Most mall managers are looking for unique
food concepts to add to their mix, and you'll enjoy a healthy
flow of foot traffic just about all year long.

=== BRIGHT IDEA ===

CRANKING OUT THE PASTA

Do you love pasta but hate the restaurant business? Restaurateurs aren't the only ones cashing in on America's pasta craze.

Paul and Diane Santillie started out making pasta as a hobby. Using a hand-cranked machine, these pastaholics would spend their weekends cranking out the stuff. At first, they made just enough to satisfy their appetites; but as their pasta's fame grew, the Santillies retired their old machine in favor of a new electric one. In 1982, they started selling packages of pasta from the Richland, Washington, gourmet and gift store where Diane worked. "Soon, Diane was producing ten to twenty pounds a day from home," says Paul.

Such productivity earned Diane the nickname "Pasta Mama"—the same name the Santillies gave to their retail operation when it opened in 1986. Since then, Pasta Mama's sales have doubled every year according to Paul, who anticipated sales of $3 million to $5 million in 1989.

Now, Pasta Mama ships over 3,000 pounds of pasta daily, in over forty-three varieties and thirty-two flavors, to specialty retailers nationwide.

=== BRIGHT IDEA ===

USING THE OL' NOODLE

Fast-food pasta operations are nothing new, but thanks to entrepreneur Albert Chi Chi, they may become faster than ever. Chi Chi is the inventor of the Pasta Mobile, a freestanding pasta restaurant that promises to give the old hot dog stand a run for its money.

Chi Chi owned an Italian restaurant until 1979, when he started Chi Chi Manufacturing Co./A.C. Enterprises, a company that built carousel units for vendors to take to carnivals and fairs. "While running the carousel business, I read an article in the food section of the local paper that said pasta was the perfect food for today's lifestyle. The author wondered why there weren't pasta stands on the street instead of hot dog stands," Chi Chi says. "So I decided to combine my two specialties."

Chi Chi created a mobile 8- by 10-foot-square concession stand, large enough to hold three people, yet small enough to be pulled behind a car. "The Pasta Mobiles are designed for use on streets, at carnivals and fairs, car shows—anywhere concession stands are permitted," says Chi Chi.

Chi Chi began his Pasta Mobile operation in October 1988. He sold his first four units by the end of that year, and has since received many more orders. Chi Chi hopes Pasta Mobiles will catch on across the country. As far as he's concerned, "There's nothing else like it."

GOURMET POTATO RESTAURANT

High Net Profit Before Taxes:	$78,000-plus
Average Net Profit Before Taxes:	$50,000
Minimum Start-up:	$75,000
Average Start-up:	$110,000

Most of us don't associate the words "gourmet" and "potato," but given the recent boom in specialty potato restaurants, that kind of thinking may be on its way out. Our research uncovered gourmet potatoes selling for up to $15 apiece in high-class specialty restaurants catering to potato lovers.

At these prices, you won't be dishing up ordinary spuds. Gourmet potatoes come stuffed with cheese, tomatoes, spinach, sautéed chicken, chili, or even caviar. Baked potatoes aren't the only option: French fries have gone upscale as well. French-fries-only stands are cropping up in malls across the country.

This trend is not surprising. Surely the average American consumer would rather try a well-dressed potato than, say, raw fish. For the entrepreneur, potatoes offer more than a palatable opportunity. Potatoes and most stuffings are low-cost items, frequently with high markups.

Upscale potato restaurants can gross as much as

$750,000; gross sales in simpler take-out potato shops with limited seating ranged from $180,000 to $350,000. Sharp management and low product costs can yield net profits of $36,000 to $75,000 or more. And well-run places have done that in the first year.

Good-bye, Potato Famine

The average American eats a whopping 118 pounds of potatoes each year—boiled, fried, mashed, and baked. For years, the potato had a rather unglamorous image. People called it starchy, fattening, bland. Now, nutritionists are hailing the potato as a prime source of vitamins, potassium, fiber, and carbohydrates. And at about 100 calories per medium potato, they can hardly be called fattening.

Hence, the potato makes a cheap, healthy, and satisfying alternative to traditional fast food. Some of the most successful potato operations are fast-food stands, usually set up in shopping malls. Most emphasize either gourmet french fries (drenched in gravy or smothered in cheese) or stuffed baked potatoes. Operations of this type are small—usually between 300 and 550 square feet—with the production area occupying virtually all of the space. From the counter, passersby can see and smell the potatoes being made—often advertisement enough to make a sale.

In these types of operations, heavy foot traffic is a must. Finding a spot in a mall food court is the best alternative. Strip centers, downtown spots, and other highly trafficked locations are also good bets. Don't make the mistake of setting up shop in a remote or inconvenient location. To achieve a high volume, you'll need to bring in impulse business.

If fast food doesn't appeal to you, consider opening a full-scale potato restaurant. Though these are less common than their fast-food counterparts, several gourmet potato restaurants are up and thriving. The trick, according to one successful operator we found, is emphasizing the healthfulness of the food. He passes out flyers at health clubs and weight salons promoting the low-calorie, high-nutrient value of potatoes—a fine alternative to regular restaurant fare.

Potatoes may be hot today, but what about tomorrow? Is this just another passing food fad? Probably not. Unlike many other recent fads, the gourmet potato is based on a perennial favorite. Americans have been eating potatoes for centuries, and will probably continue to do so for years to come. To make sure you capitalize on that future business, however, you'll need to practice sound management, planning, and promotion.

======================= BRIGHT IDEA =======================

SPECIALTY OF THE HOUSE

Maine has its lobsters, Maryland its soft-shell crabs. In San Francisco, tourists clamor for sourdough bread, and in New York a favorite delicacy is pizza. Even small towns have their signature foods. In Gilroy, California, that food is garlic.

Every summer, Gilroy sponsors a garlic festival that draws upwards of 140,000 people from around the world. In a city that proclaims itself the garlic capital of the world, an unusual store called Garlic World is the culinary center of town. The 10,000-square-foot store sells garlic-flavored foods, fruits, vegetables, dried fruits, juices, and local wines. "Many of these can't be found at local grocery stores," says Carolyn Tognetti, co-owner of the shop.

The business began as a roadside fruit stand, operated for seventeen years by the Tognetti family. The Garlic World store opened in March 1986 when the Tognettis and partner Don Christopher decided to bring the seasonal business indoors. With sales of $1.3 million for 1989, Garlic World has become so popular that the owners are thinking of adding on a restaurant serving garlic-related foods next door.

Though your hometown may not be renowned for one particular food, you may still start a successful specialty food shop. Consider a shop devoted to exotic spices, ethnic foods, out-of-town items, or gourmet fare. Just remember to match the specialty to your local market, and make sure that you offer something that regular supermarkets do not. As Garlic World proves, with the right mix of creativity and palatability, even a common kitchen staple can be the basis for a gourmet business.

ICE CREAM STORE

High Net Profit Before Taxes:	$77,000
Average Net Profit Before Taxes:	$50,000
Minimum Start-up:	$48,500
Average Start-up:	$70,000

The American craving for ice cream accounts for some 900 million gallons annually—far more than an occasional midnight snack. Though ice cream stores are nothing new, they are back and better than ever.

Entrepreneurs around the country are grossing $50,000 to $80,000 yearly out of small shops. These are not limited to the familiar pink-and-white-striped shops we all grew up with. Today's ice cream parlors heap on the atmosphere, be that down-home and funky or upscale and trendy. The ice cream is anything but ordinary, too. Our researchers have spotted unusual flavors ranging from raspberry chocolate truffle to chocolate chip cookie dough.

Cream of the Crop

Just a decade or so ago, ice cream was ice cream. You bought it in half-gallon blocks at the supermarket and ate it with birthday cake. Today, ice cream is a culinary experience. It's made with cream, whole eggs, fresh fruit, imported chocolate, and other premium ingredients by small companies and individual shops.

The difference is tremendous. Mass-produced ice cream may contain a host of chemicals, including ammonium caseinate (also used in varnish), diethyl glucol (also used in car radiators), and butraldehyde (used in rubber cement, but tastes like walnuts). All told, about 1,600 chemicals are FDA-approved for use in ice cream. Not surprisingly, natural food buffs aren't ecstatic about consuming these chemicals. And what's more, neither are true ice cream aficionados. All natural, superpremium ice cream not only sounds better, it tastes better as well.

In fact, it's this high-quality segment of the ice cream market that's growing the fastest. Better still, superpremium ice cream represents a niche that's still accessible to the small operator. Ice-cream consumers now equate small with quality. All you have to do is live up to the image.

Standards Are High

Considering that Americans eat about 15 quarts of ice cream per person per year, finding a good market for your ice-cream shop shouldn't be hard. Though just about anyone is a potential customer, the primary market for super-premium ice cream is 12- to 19-year-olds and 23- to 37-year-olds. Locating near a college campus is usually a good bet. If you don't live near a college, look for a location with a dense concentration of people within one to three miles of your shop. Heavy foot traffic is a must.

Beyond location, the quality of your ice cream is critical. By all means, don't skimp. Successful entrepreneurs have discovered that the more outrageous the flavors, the better. Standards are high in today's market. Even supermarkets carry Häagen-Dazs and other superpremium brands. Aim high with your products. Consumers will drive miles for a superior dish of ice cream, but you'll be lucky to draw your next-door neighbor with a mediocre scoop.

Also concentrate on promoting your business. Well-placed ads and local publicity are both valuable, as are conspicuous signs to bring in street traffic. Bring in customers with offbeat contests, drawings, entertainment, and other attention-grabbers. Make your shop a fun place to visit as well as a good source of ice cream.

=========== BRIGHT IDEA ===========

BROWN-BAGGING IT

Can't afford a facility to launch your new food business? Rent someone else's. "Many tavern owners and supper clubs only use their kitchens during the evening," explains Jerri George, cofounder of Wee-Bag-It Delivery Emporiums, a Florida-based food-delivery franchise. "A well-equipped commercial kitchen can do double duty during the daytime, at the lunch hour. We are a one-of-a-kind franchise, targeted at the business-to-business market. We deliver upscale breakfasts and lunches to corporate clients."

With seven franchises in Florida, Wee-Bag-It has stream-lined its lunch menu, focusing on items that travel well. Co-owners Fred and Jerri George and Tom and Susan Maguire deliver stuffed baked potatoes, Caesar and Waldorf salads, and a variety of sandwiches for company executives who prefer to dine in for lunch.

Some Wee-Bag-It franchisees are restaurant owners seek-ing to expand their businesses; others simply rent their commercial kitchens from existing businesses during hours when the kitchens aren't in use. Either way, both the restau-rant and the delivery service benefit from reduced overhead and increased profits.

═══════════════ BRIGHT IDEA ═══════════════

HAPPY SNAILS TO YOU

Perhaps you're like Lucy Ricardo of *I Love Lucy* fame. When she inadvertently ordered escargots at a Parisian restaurant, she screamed out loud at the sight of cooked snails on her plate. But not everyone is this squeamish. In fact, there are enough escargot connoisseurs out there to make snails a $200 million product internationally.

Who's eating them? Increasingly, Americans are. Though snails are catching on rather slowly (dare we say at a snail's pace?), some entrepreneurs are anticipating a boom. Accord-ing to Ralph Tucker, snail farmer and president of the Snail Club of America, snail ranches are a popular entrepreneurial venture—and they grow more popular by the day. Raised on a healthy diet of lettuce, corn meal, and water, farm-fresh snails taste a far sight better than the canned variety, mak-ing them a hot commodity at gourmet restaurants.

And they're healthy, too. Whether you like them or not, snails are good for you. They have no fat, no cholesterol, and are loaded with nutrients. Drop them into a pot of boiling

water with a little lemon juice for three minutes, and they
pop out of their shells succulent, tender, and delicious (well,
at least 9 percent of the population thinks so).

FLAME-BROILED CHICKEN
RESTAURANT

High Net Profit Before Taxes:	$120,000
Average Net Profit Before Taxes:	$90,000
Minimum Start-up:	$75,500
Average Start-up:	$120,000

There are more ways to cook a chicken than deep-fat frying
it. In today's health-conscious society, fried chicken is considered by many to be downright sinful. New, healthier alternatives are sought—and found—at the nation's flame-broiled
chicken take-out restaurants.

Marinated, grilled chicken is an ideal fast food. Prepared
with a Mexican flair, it's exotic and different. It's different
from the usual fried fare, yet simple enough to feed to finicky
kids. It is also cheap and easy to prepare.

Major chains such as El Pollo Loco in Southern California
and El Pollo Asado in Arizona—as well as independents nationwide—are popularizing Mexican-style grilled chicken.
Though the main concentration of these operations continues to be in the Southwest, they are rapidly expanding
into northern territories.

What Sizzles

Charbroiled chicken sales represent about 3 percent of
the fast-food chicken market, but proprietors expect this to
change. The potential for growth in this segment is great,
and smart operators are eager to capitalize—largely through
franchising.

The simplicity of the chicken makes it universally appealing. Whole chickens are butterflied, then soaked in a citrus-
based marinade overnight. They are then grilled (usually
over a gas grill), basted, and cut into serving pieces. Accom-

paniments usually include Mexican-style rice, beans, steamed tortillas, salsa, guacamole, and various salads (cole slaw, potato salad, etc.). Sometimes, flame-broiled chicken outfits also feature simple dishes like burritos, tacos, and tostados.

The Mexican flavor of this product makes it a natural for Hispanic areas, but people in the field believe this product easily cuts across demographic lines. In fact, if you're considering a shop in an unadventuresome area, you can serve the same product with tamer side dishes and call it "American charbroiled chicken."

Simple Set-up

Most pollo operations are modeled after fast-food joints, emphasizing take-out and serve-yourself seating. A take-out-only operation can be set up in as little as 500 square feet, though many charbroiled chicken restaurants do offer some informal seating. In warm climates, a patio or outside seating area works nicely. If you plan to include a seating area, 1,500 to 2,000 square feet should be ample space.

The location of your pollo restaurant can make or break your business. Convenience is key, so watch for high visibility and easy access from the street, as well as plenty of parking. Also pay close attention to the surrounding neighborhood. Office buildings will provide a steady lunch trade, while a more residential setting will bring in dinner and weekend traffic. Ideally, your location will offer both.

Equipment requirements for a fast-food chicken restaurant are relatively simple. In addition to basics like cash registers and counters, you will need a flame-broiler (gas-fed grills are most common, but brick and wood-burning metal ovens are also available), a walk-in cooler, a tortilla steamer, and possibly a deep-fat fryer for french fries and tortilla chips. Unless you have vast experience in fast-food operations, consult a fast-food facilities design company or restaurant equipment dealer for individual help.

Under sharp management, a pollo operation can serve up to 300 chickens on a weekend day. The manager of a successful franchise outlet told us he serves 200 chickens on a bad day. Gross sales per day can run between $1,000 and

$3,000—with net profit before taxes between 20 and 25 percent.

======================= BRIGHT IDEA =======================

DINNER IS SERVED

Besides having a phone in your golf bag, having a personal chef is the ultimate luxury. Now that luxury is available from the Epicurean Connection in West Hollywood, California. The cost? $500 to $700 per week.

A professional home-chef placement firm launched by Susan Rabb and Shelley Janson, the Epicurean Connection provides clients with gourmet chefs who are skilled enough to cook meals fit for the best restaurants.

Janson, also the owner of the Epicurean Cooking School, came up with the idea when she started getting calls from celebrities disgruntled with standard domestic placement agencies. "They would call me for recommendations after having lost their own chefs, but I was too busy to help them," she says.

So she teamed up with Rabb, a former advertising executive, and the two created the new business. Today, placing chefs in private homes is a full-time job for both. "We hear from new clients every day," says Rabb. "And we've worked with some of the top names in the entertainment industry."

BAKERY

High Net Profit Before Taxes:	$115,000
Average Net Profit Before Taxes:	$70,000
Minimum Start-up:	$83,000
Average Start-up:	$134,000

Man does not live by bread alone. He also consumes a lot of cakes, cookies, croissants, brownies, brioches, tarts, pies, tortes, and cupcakes. Bakeries are among the oldest food businesses operating today, yet they never seem to get stale.

Even in a society obsessed with counting calories, a good bakery can serve up toothsome profits.

Yet this is no place for the run-of-the-mill. Imagination is key in today's bakery business. Our researchers uncovered a host of interesting concepts, from gourmet loaves to X-rated cakes. Ethnic bakeries are on the rise, and ethnics aren't the only ones lining up for bagels, foccacia, bao, and gulab jamun. The multicultural marketplace seems to welcome exotic tastes. Upscale is also here to stay. While pricey goods aren't necessarily best, a plain old cake won't sell like a Kahlua, poppyseed, or French chocolate one will.

Today, the bakery business is anything but on the wane. But to thrive in a competitive environment, today's baker has to be smart. Excellent products, smart management, and a keen knowledge of the market are essentials.

Your Slice of the Market

A successful bakery starts with the right mix of customers. Before opening your doors, check the demographics of your area to determine what people might buy (and whether they will buy at all). Singles and young married people in their twenties and thirties are a prime market, as are older consumers.

Check the local supermarket to see what they sell. What kinds of breads move fast? Which end up on the day-old shelf? Does the supermarket bake its own cakes and pies, or is its selection limited to commercial brands and frozen goods? What kinds of goods do they offer? And how will you entice customers away from their products?

Again, quality and distinctiveness are the answers. At Sweet Stuff in Biloxi, Mississippi, custom-made cakes are the specialty of the house. Co-owners Mary Vuyovich and June Ford have baked cakes in the shapes of guitars, trucks, and video-game aliens. Their three-tiered champagne cake has a real bottle of champagne designed into it. According to Vuyovich and Ford, going the extra mile is a must in a rural community like theirs. "To attract customers to our shop, we figured we'd better offer them something special and out of the ordinary," says Vuyovich.

Cakes are just one facet of the bakery business. One store

we investigated sells nothing but gourmet bread, including
rich rye loaves and crisp, light French rolls. Another bakery
we found sells only chocolate desserts—mousses, tortes,
cakes, and shortbreads. Whatever your specialty, just remember that a bakery depends on its ability to lure customers away from grocery store goods. Your products have to be
worth the extra time and money consumers must spend to
get them.

A Piece of Cake

Bakeries thrive in all kinds of locations. Foot traffic is a
plus, so mall spots and downtown areas are good choices.
This is especially true if you're selling impulse items like
cookies. Strip centers are another good choice, provided they
have ample parking. You might also consider opening your
shop near a supermarket that does not have an on-site bakery. That way, customers can pick up a quick dessert or loaf
of bread on their way home from the market.

Because most bakery items are inexpensive, you'll depend
on volume for profits. Most successful bakeries do not rely on
heavy advertising to bring in customers. Convenience and
word-of-mouth are your most important marketing tools.
With shrewd management and a good reputation, a bakery
can enjoy profits of over $100,000 a year.

===================== BRIGHT IDEA =====================

POURING IT ON

What's hotter than the average briquet? Gourmet barbecue
sauce—especially if it comes from the kitchens of America's
entrepreneurs. Although major brands like Heinz and Hunt's
still account for most of the market, boutique labels like
Maull's, Gayle's, and Wild West Gourmet are finding their way
onto grocers' shelves.

Take the case of Dan Morrow, founder of Wild West Foods,
Inc. in Phoenix, Arizona. Dissatisfied with the bland barbecue sauces available on store shelves, Morrow set out to

create a unique barbecue sauce. But he refused to read any recipes or look at ingredient labels on existing barbecue sauces. Instead, every night for three months, he cooked and tasted batches of homemade barbecue sauce until he created one that he liked. "I tried it out on some of my friends, and they really liked it," says Morrow. That was when he decided the sauce had sales potential.

Working from his Phoenix kitchen, Morrow bottled two cases of his Wild West Gourmet Barbecue Sauce and began peddling it to local stores in July 1988. Before he knew it, Morrow had sold his barbecue sauce to more than forty independent grocers. And after finding a manufacturer, Morrow was able to place his sauce in ABCO stores, a major Arizona food chain. During the peak barbecue season—Easter through Labor Day—Morrow delivers an average of more than 200 cases a month.

2

PERSONAL SERVICES

BRIGHT IDEA

SPECIAL DAY CARE

Kids with working moms all need day care, but some kids need special attention more than others. Developmentally disabled children and children with serious illnesses often don't fit into regular day-care programs.

With this in mind, Santa Ana, California, entrepreneurs Jeff Gasser and Julia Bell founded the Kangaroo Kids Center for Fragile Children in 1989. "We designed the center to serve as an alternative to home nursing and hospitals for children who need special care," explains Gasser. "For example, we care for children with cancer and children who need oxygen."

Caring for such children in a day-care center as opposed to a home has several advantages for both children and their parents. "The center costs an average of 40 percent less than home nursing, and allows insurance benefits to be used for future illnesses [instead of for nursing expenses]," says Gasser. "In addition to the lower cost, the day-care center is far more valuable developmentally for the kids because they are stimulated instead of being isolated."

Gasser and Bell are benefiting, too. Gasser says Kangaroo Kids began turning a profit after just four months of operations. "Not only that," he adds, "but people are calling us from all over the country about starting their own [similar] day-care centers."

SINGULAR SENSATIONS

According to the U.S. Census Bureau, some 66 million Americans over 18 are unmarried. That's more than one-third of the adult population. While these figures bode well for the nation's dating services, they also bring good news to other businesses that cater specifically to singles.

Single Scene is a Scottsdale, Arizona, newspaper geared toward the singles market. According to editor Janet Jacobsen, singles are eager for new, inexpensive ways to meet potential mates. Each issue of *Single Scene* costs 75 cents and contains roughly 300 personal ads. Monthly newsstand circulation: 7,500.

For the more technically advanced, there is New York City entrepreneur Barry Kush's service, SingleFax. Kush introduces eligible mates to one another via facsimile machines. "When fax machines become as commonplace as the VCR, singles everywhere will communicate by fax," predicts Kush, who charges $50 for his service.

Even the most general information can be useful to singles. Rodger Doyle, president of Map Makers in Kenmore, New York, has compiled a color-coded singles map, selling for $9.95, that pinpoints the ratio of single men to single women in 150 major metropolitan areas of the U.S.

BRIDAL CONSULTING

Most brides will tell you it's a long walk to the altar. Long before strains of Wagner accompany that all-important stroll down the aisle, the bride spends months planning the ceremony, arranging the reception, and undergoing more stress than the average astronaut. And since more and more brides work, the hassle of planning a wedding is magnified. For many, having someone else do the legwork is worth almost any amount of money—and that's good news for America's bridal consultants.

American couples spent more than $27 billion on weddings in 1988, and the bridal consultant is sharing a larger piece of the pie each year. The return to big, traditional weddings has brought with it the problem of staging this complex event. Busy couples are saving time and headaches by delegating problems to the wedding planner.

New Look for an Old Business

In Victorian times, wedding planners helped brides sort through the maze of social customs that surrounded a proper wedding. Today, a good bridal consultant can still offer advice on etiquette, but that's just the tip of the iceberg. One of the most important services a consultant can provide is access to the best vendors. This gives couples a leg up on finding the perfect site, the most lavish flowers, and the right caterer.

In contrast to their Victorian counterparts, today's planners stress individuality, not propriety. Though big weddings are back, they aren't necessarily following Emily Post to the letter. Successful consultants work with clients to create unique events—even if that means fulfilling unusual requests. Another facet of the consultant's duties: budgeting. A savvy consultant should be able to work within any budget, and help clients get the most for their money.

Start with Research

You can start a wedding consultant business with less than $7,000. But don't let the low investment fool you: This is not a get-rich-quick business.

To be a good consultant, you must do your homework. The first step is locating good, reliable vendors. Visit all the local sites; consult with every florist, photographer, stationer, videographer, disc jockey, and band in your area. Be sure to check references for every vendor you contact. The more thoroughly researched your list of vendors, the more valuable it is.

In addition to research, you'll need patience. Bridal consultants don't advertise through the usual media. Referral is the primary method of getting the word out. This kind of advertising is cheap, but it is not fast. Many consultants recommend starting the business part-time while working at a regular job. In time, your business will grow into a full-time venture, but in the meantime, you can rely on an outside means of support.

Blissful Profits

Though prices and methods of billing vary, $2,500 is not unheard of for planning a major event. Some planners charge a percentage of the overall budget, typically 15 percent. Since many traditional weddings today cost upwards of $10,000, the consultant earns $1,500 or more. Other planners charge flat fees of $1,000 or more, depending on the services rendered.

Additionally, you may also collect commissions from vendors. This way, you can charge your clients less and still bring in a tidy profit. On the other hand, vendors may give you lower priority if you're paying less for their services than their other customers.

Established wedding consultants bring in net profits as high as $123,000, though the average full-time operation probably nets closer to $57,000. For many veteran planners, the financial rewards aren't the only compensation. The creativity and excitement of planning the perfect wedding is also a source of bliss.

====== BRIGHT IDEA ======

PET-ZERCISE

The health and fitness craze that has swept America over the past few decades may soon hit a new market. Sure, you're in top shape, but how about your schnauzer? It's no joke: Judith Langer, president of New York City-based research firm Langer Associates, Inc., predicts that pet exercise equipment and gyms are the next step pet owners will take in their quest to keep their animal companions healthy.

"Studies we've done on pet owners show that there is a lot of concern with their pets' health," says Langer. "Many dog owners feel that they aren't doing enough for their dogs in terms of exercise." Langer believes it's only a matter of time until entrepreneurs begin taking advantage of the untapped market for pet exercise services.

But before you run out and invest in canine saunas, stationary bikes, and weight equipment, check your local market. Stephe Marquart, owner and operator of Coast Canine Country Club in Santa Ana Heights, California, thinks canine fitness programs must be suited to specific markets. Though Coast Canine Country Club does offer swimming pools and dog runs for the dogs that board there, the kennel is not a health club. "New York City is definitely a place that would need dog exercising services," says Marquart, "but there wouldn't really be a market for that kind of service anywhere people have yards for their dogs to run in."

Still, no one wants a paunchy pooch, and leisure time continues to dwindle. Will Sparky be condemned to a life of inactivity? Or will Mom and Dad come through with a personal trainer? Clearly, this isn't a service for every market. But given the right combination of demographics and marketing, pet-zercise could be the wave of the future.

===== BRIGHT IDEA =====

RIDING THE GRAVY TRAIN

For handicapped and elderly people, even the simplest tasks—like climbing up the stairs or going to the supermarket—can turn into major challenges. Under these circumstances, carrying a fifty-pound sack of dog food is just about out of the question.

Matthew Hallisey, owner of Animal Express in Wethersfield, Connecticut, understands how heavy and awkward a large bag of dog food can be. In fact, that's one of the reasons he started his dog- and cat-food delivery company in March, 1989.

"The major thrust behind Animal Express is convenience," Hallisey says. "Buying food for the family pet can be a huge hassle for people who are incapacitated or who simply don't have the time to stop at the pet store. We think it's a great service to the elderly, the handicapped, and families with working adults."

Hallisey caters to his list of clients by arranging convenient pick-up and delivery times at different locations. Animal Express purchases pet food at wholesale prices so the customer pays only the retail price with no extra delivery charge. "I buy only the best food for the animals, and I sell it at prices that are competitive with those of the retail locations in the area," Hallisey says.

Future plans include opening a retail location from which the Animal Express delivery operation will run. At this point, however, Animal Express is run out of a warehouse in Wethersfield. Hallisey predicts, "Our pet-food delivery service will be an outstanding complement to a retail location."

MOBILE DISC-JOCKEY SERVICE

How would you like Benny Goodman, Frank Sinatra, Madonna, or Michael Jackson to entertain at your next party? A mobile DJ can make it happen—and for a fraction of what a good local band would cost. DJs aren't just for high-school sock hops anymore. Party hosts of every sort are discovering this inexpensive alternative to live music.

Disc jockeys started out spinning records at parties in the fifties and sixties, then evolved to new heights during the pinnacle of the disco era in the late seventies and early eighties. Disco died, but the DJ concept didn't. The DJ business is a multi-million-dollar industry these days—and it hasn't stopped growing yet.

From Humble Beginnings

You needn't be a music mogul to break into this business. With some basic stereo equipment, a collection of records, transportation, a few sharp outfits, and a good musical ear, you could get started on a small scale working weekends.

One operator we talked to started his DJ service while still in high school. At first, his service amounted to bringing a stereo and records to local parties. But eventually, he started doing wedding receptions. Now, they're the bulk of his business.

Since prime party hours are on weekends, you won't have to quit your regular job to become a DJ. An investment of $5,000 should buy you enough equipment and inventory to put you in business, especially if you already have transportation and a sizable record collection to start. A good DJ has all the latest tunes, so be prepared to spend about $1,000 upgrading your current selection.

As far as equipment goes, most mobile DJs use a dual turntable system with headphones. As one song is playing, the master of music cues up the next tune without missing a beat. Because many albums only have one hit song on them, some disc jockeys rely on 45s or individually prerecorded party tapes with a run of top songs. Some DJs swear by high-fidelity, compact, durable CDs. With a fair initial investment, you can use all three formats: albums, CDs, and cassettes.

Expansion Possibilities

How much can a good disc jockey earn? Depending on your community, the going rate ranges from $50 to $250 per hour, plus tips. Rates climb as more extras are included: Bubble machines, strobe lights, fog machines, and sophisticated light shows all jack up the prices.

Full-time disc jockeys with aggressive marketing can earn more than $25,000 annually by working at least three gigs a weekend. But this is difficult to do. Remember that your business is restricted to party hours—and generally that means weekends only. Typically, working as a disc jockey provides a steady secondary income, not a primary income. However, it's not impossible to expand your concept.

With proper marketing, your service can grow into a veritable party machine. We found one owner who employs more than 200 part-time DJs and works over 12,000 parties in nine states each year. His gross sales are $3 million. "You don't have to be good-looking or beautiful [to be a DJ]," he says. "You don't have to be Mr. or Ms. Personality. You just need warmth and rhythm. You need to enjoy being in front of people."

================= BRIGHT IDEA =================

HOUSESITTING SERVICE

For starting a business, there's no place like home—even if it's someone else's. Housesitting services are sweeping the nation. Providing everything from hourly service (to let in carpet cleaners, plumbers, and cable TV repair people) to monthly live-in care, housesitters are greeting an eager market.

Services vary depending on the owner's goals. Some housesitters don't charge for their services. Instead, they live rent-free (often in ritzy quarters) at their clients' homes. Communities with large summer-vacation populations are ideal for this kind of business. Families use their vacation homes for three months out of the year, then hire a service to watch that home for the remaining nine months. Another lucrative market is real estate. An empty home takes longer to sell, and may be subject to insurance snags. By hiring a live-in sitter, the owner solves both problems—and usually at little or no cost.

You can make money running an in-home service by marketing your services to potential clients, then recruiting a crew of sitters to fill the vacancies. You may either collect a fee from clients or from the sitters themselves, who pay you a small finder's fee in lieu of rent.

Other options include drop-in and hourly service. Drop-in sitters come by occasionally to pick up mail, water plants, turn lights on and off, and check for any calamities (broken pipes, caved-in roofs). If pets are involved, they may come by as often as twice a day to see that the brood is fed, watered, exercised, and healthy. Hourly sitters come by just to let in delivery or repair people while clients are at work. Of course, you can combine drop-in and hourly services, and even act as an agent for live-in care to boot. The options are virtually limitless.

A simple office (perhaps a spare bedroom at home) is all you need to establish a housesitting service. To reach potential housesitters, place ads in local and campus newspapers and post flyers on campus bulletin boards. Screen applicants carefully. The crucial trait that you're looking for is responsibility. Ask applicants if they have pets and if they've ever cared for a house. Contact their former employers for references. Then have the selected applicants bonded by an insurance company.

If you plan to offer drop-in or hourly service yourself, your main tools will be transportation and a telephone. Since this business usually requires that you work seven days a week (including holidays), you may want to hire part-time help once your volume picks up.

BALLOON DELIVERY SERVICE

High Net Profit Before Taxes:	$100,000
Average Net Profit Before Taxes:	$20,000
Minimum Start-up:	$600
Average Start-up:	$8,000

Flowers again? Today's busy lifestyles don't allow much time for gift shopping, so many people send a nice bouquet instead of a gift. But sooner or later, the old flower trick gets old. What's as convenient and thoughtful as sending flowers, but more imaginative and fun?

Balloons fit the bill. "Ballooning" friends (and enemies) has become a favorite form of communication. And bouquet deliveries are only part of the story. Decorating with elaborate balloon sculptures and arches at parties and weddings has also grown in popularity. And with proper management, the profits can be equally festive—as high as $100,000 annually.

Better still, start-up costs are minimal. A helium tank, string, balloons, and a reliable car are about all you need to get started. You can even launch the business from your home, then move to a business location when volume increases.

A Bunch of Options

There's more than one way to profit in the balloon business. One popular service is balloon delivery, in which helium-filled balloons are arranged in custom assortments and delivered to a specific location. This is not strictly a balloon-vending operation, but a service-oriented business requiring reliability and style. It does not, however, require a high-volume location. A phone is all you need.

Balloon delivery also calls for a certain measure of creativity. Some operations make real bouquets out of balloons; others attach baskets to their balloons (à la the hot-air variety), and fill the baskets with champagne, chocolates, or other small gifts. Stuffed animals and coffee mugs are other popular options. Costumed delivery people can also make a splash, especially if you add a celebratory song and dance to the mix.

Another angle of this business is party and special-event decoration. Balloons as decorations have been taking the country by storm in the past few years, and there is no sign of letup. According to one professional, balloons can define a space in ways that flowers can't. In fact, wherever flowers can be used for decorating, generally balloons can, too.

Opening a retail location is another idea to explore. Naturally, maintaining a storefront is significantly more expensive than operating out of a warehouse. On the other hand, successful retail operations have opened up around the country specializing in balloons and related cards, gifts, and candy.

Not All Fun and Games

The balloon business is unquestionably fun, but it's also a serious undertaking. In the past decade, the competition has increased. Successful balloon businesses rely on careful planning, efficient marketing, and excellent customer service. Learning to cultivate all your potential markets—from individual gift-givers to restaurants and hotels in need of striking decoration—will be a major factor in your success.

========== BRIGHT IDEA ==========

MASSAGE AND MEAL

As if a gourmet meal weren't enough, Matthew Sarver and Amy Tunick also offer their clients professional massages. Sarver and Tunick are cofounders of Pamper & Dine, a new Studio City, California-based mobile massage and catering service.

The unlikely combination of services came about by marriage. Sarver and Tunick wanted to start a new venture together. She's a trained masseuse; he's an expert chef. "Our most monumental concern was finding a name for the business," says Tunick. "Once we did that, we were ready to go."

The packages, which range from $300 to $500, are like a dream come true for stressed-out working couples. "I prepare a pre-arranged gourmet meal while Amy massages each member of the couple for a half-hour," explains Sarver. "By the time the massage is complete, the couple's meal is ready to go." The clients, however, are a different story. Says Sarver: "Most of our clients fall asleep during the massage."

========== BRIGHT IDEA ==========

KIDDIE CLIPPERS

Watching the World Series and cutting hair just don't mix. After a baseball-loving barber mangled her son's hair by trimming it with one eye on the TV set, Geri Bemrick decided it was time someone opened a hair salon exclusively for children. E.J.'s Little People opened in Fair Oaks, California, in

1974, and in spite of skepticism from her colleagues, Bemrick now has nine locations in California, with her tenth on the way.

Bemrick started on a shoestring with only $5,000 and has never borrowed a dime to start a store. "[This strategy] makes your growth slow, but it also makes it orderly," she says.

E.J.'s prices are moderate—from $7 to $16. "I like to deal with the McDonald's audience—I want to attract bigger numbers [of clients]," she says. "I look at it as a service to the community."

Of the nine E.J.'s stores in operation, no two look alike. For one of her stores, Bemrick cruised auto wrecking yards and lugged home heaps of grilles, tires, mirrors—even a whole Volkswagen Rabbit, which she sawed in half and used for seating in the reception area. Her "circus" store, which took eight months to complete, features authentic carousel animals, and her barnyard salon is complete with yellow straw. Hand-painted murals add vibrant color and interest to the walls.

Sitting still is crucial for a good cut, so busy surroundings give the hairdresser a psychological edge. Getting a talking mynah bird to say a word or two, or pointing out tiny lifelike mice climbing up the pipes keeps the kids' minds on fun and off the shearing. Bemrick's staff is specially trained before they're allowed on the floor. "Kids spit and scream and bite," exclaims Bemrick, "so my staff has to be better than average."

========= BRIGHT IDEA =========

TRAVELING TRESSES

Why should salespeople have the lock on mobile businesses? Raymond MacNeil of Halifax, Nova Scotia, is a traveling hairstylist. Not only does mobility make the job infinitely more interesting, but it's good for business, too.

Using a car in the winter and a motorcycle in the summer,

the 29-year-old hairstylist tools around from one locale to another to do everything from cuts and colors to perms and weaves. "I've cut hair on a catwalk high above a construction site," he laughs. "I've styled hair at the offices of businessmen and doctors. I've even gone to the beach and created a hairstyle right there on the sand."

MacNeil got the idea for his flexible, virtually overhead-free business in 1984, when he read an article about a mobile hairstylist in London. In 1986, he hit the road full-time, and he's never looked back.

"I love my work, and business is getting better and better every day," says MacNeil. "I'm twice as busy now as I was last year at this time, and by next year, I hope to be four times as busy as I am now."

DATING SERVICE

High Net Profit Before Taxes:	$75,000-plus
Average Net Profit Before Taxes:	$50,000
Minimum Start-up:	$25,000
Average Start-up:	$40,000

Of all the horrors life inflicts on us, few are more painful than the wasted date. You know from the moment your eyes meet that it's all wrong. He arrives at your door wearing a "No Fat Chicks" T-shirt. She has arranged for her great-aunt to join you. You can't agree on anything—religion, politics, marriage, vegetables. In a single evening, you have wasted stacks of money, hours of valuable time, not to mention the disappointment you've suffered. And yet, even dating the wrong person seems better than not dating anyone at all.

Welcome to the world of modern dating. Why is finding a mate so difficult these days? Leisure time is at a premium. Working people who don't have time for a good dinner certainly don't have time to meet and screen potential mates. Many single people are transplants from other areas and don't have established social networks through which to be "fixed up." Outlets for meeting new people are limited, whether you're too cynical for church or too innocent for nightclubs. And besides, these days the stakes are high. Singles have strong notions about compatibility. They want mates with similar values, professional aspirations, family goals, and personal interests.

Given these constraints, how can any of America's 66 million single adults find a mate? The fact is, many don't. Many others realize they need help. And that's precisely what they get through a dating service.

The Changing Scene

When dating services emerged in the sixties, they were considered something of a joke. Matching couples by computer seemed the worst kind of gimmick. But that image is changing. Contemporary dating services don't offer magic formulas—just legitimate help. Personal service and a professional attitude are often more important than a load of equipment.

For new operators with limited funds, this comes as good news. By keeping your costs to a minimum, you can launch a dating service for as little as $25,000—or even less. One company we found was started from home for less than $5,000. In its fourth year of business, it was grossing in the $80,000 to $100,000 range. Because operations were simple, profit margins were between 25 and 30 percent. In this case, the yield was $20,000 to $30,000 net pretax, before the owner's salary.

There are several formats a dating service can take. The simplest rely on short questionnaires and personal instinct for matchmaking. Others are more technology-oriented. Though computer dating has lost some of its fad appeal, computers are still deemed useful for matching couples by age, profession, political orientation, personal interests, religion, height, or any of a variety of variables. Video dating has also gained in popularity, since it allows clients to screen potential dates confidentially. Some dating services don't stress dating at all: Marriage is the ultimate goal, and it's pursued with a vengeance. The fees are higher, but then so are the stakes.

Location First

You'll need a fairly large population base to start a successful dating service. Insiders recommend locating in a metropolitan area with at least 500,000 people. Also consider local demographics. Liberal, cosmopolitan types are more likely to use a dating service than conservative folks. And middle- or upper-middle-class singles are usually the best prospects.

===================== BRIGHT IDEA =====================

CANINE CABBY

Your dog can't drive himself to the vet, so Los Angeles entrepreneur Steve May has the next best thing: Pet Limo. May, whose motto is "We escort your pet to the vet," started his pet taxi service in 1984, after a decade of working as an animal technician at a West Hollywood veterinary clinic. One year and 10,000 advertising flyers later, clients were clamoring for the Pet Limo transportation services.

Pet Limo provides emergency ambulance services as well as transportation to the vet for regular check-ups. May also offers a specialized pet travel agency service that books flights for pets, chauffeurs them to the airport, and personally makes sure they get on the plane.

For about $100 per year, May offers a membership with services like food delivery and discounts on animal trainers. May's three Pet Limo vans—equipped with TVs to relax traveling pets—grossed nearly $80,000 in 1989. Having recently completed franchise registration, May soon hopes to have franchisees spoiling pets across America.

NANNY PLACEMENT SERVICE

High Net Profit Before Taxes:	$112,380
Average Net Profit Before Taxes:	$61,464
Minimum Start-up:	$11,795
Average Start-up:	$23,375

Since the early 1980s, the number of mothers who work outside the home has increased dramatically. Currently, there are 12 million working women with children under the age of 5—more working mothers than at any other time in history. And by the turn of the century, this figure is expected to double.

With so many mothers entering the work force, the need for quality day care is also increasing. Many parents are uncomfortable with the idea of placing their children in day-care centers. In some cases, traditional day care is simply not adequate to accommodate a parent's demanding schedule. Instead, these parents are turning to nannies for help with child care.

It's no wonder, then, that nanny placement services have been steadily cropping up across the nation in the past few years. These businesses provide a valuable service to both families in need of nannies and nannies looking for families to serve. By thoroughly screening families and nannies regarding their lifestyles, habits, child-care training, and backgrounds, these agencies help make the best possible match for both parties. The placement service is usually free to nannies, but costs families an average of $750 to $1,500.

Taking Control

One reason nannies are in such demand is because parents are realizing the importance of maintaining control over their children's physical and social environment, says Jacqueline Clark, owner of A Choice Nanny, a Columbia, Maryland-based franchise company. "The best way to achieve this kind of control is to have a private child-care helper come into the home," Clark says.

Another factor is convenience. Conventional day-care services can be inflexible. For instance, many charge exorbitant penalties for watching a child "after-hours"—as much as $5 for every 15 minutes. Or, if parents are usually at work until 7:00 P.M., they may have to use two day-care providers: one between 8 A.M. and 5 P.M. and another between 5 P.M. and 7 P.M. Not only is this arrangement disruptive to the child, but it is also inconvenient and expensive for the adults.

Nannies provide parents and children with stable, reliable care. Children get more individual attention from a nanny. And parents know that if the child gets sick, or if either parent has to work late or leave town, child care won't be a problem.

The Nanny Market

"When selecting a franchise site, we study the demographics of an area to determine the percentage of professional women, number of births, and per capita income," says Clark. A Choice Nanny franchises only in areas that have at least 3,500 working women with children under the age of 6. And like most nanny services, the company's clientele consists of families from mid- to upper-income levels.

Most families that use nanny services have incomes of $75,000 and up, and the parents are usually professionals who live in affluent areas. However, some single parents and families with lower incomes are also hiring nannies so that their children can receive the best available care.

Screening Counts

To ensure the quality of care, nanny services must screen their applicants before placing them. The screening process includes checking references, medical records, and more, says Joy Wayne, owner of Nannies Plus Inc. in Livingston, New Jersey. After in-depth interviews with Nannies Plus counselors, both by phone and in person, the nannies have the opportunity to meet with several families before a placement is made.

"The nannies come to the office and meet about eight families," says Wayne. "We usually have four nannies going through the interviews on these days." Both the nannies and the families are provided with guidelines of important questions to ask in order to determine how suitable they are for one another. If a nanny and a family hit it off, the nanny will usually begin work the same day.

Calling All Nannies!

Perhaps one of the most challenging tasks facing a nanny

service today is finding experienced, responsible nannies. The demand for nannies is far greater than the supply, according to Cathie Robertson, president of the International Nanny Association (INA) in Austin, Texas. "The reality is that there just aren't enough trained nannies," she says, "so the agencies have to place nannies based on their life experiences."

One problem is logistics. To be successful, a nanny service must set up shop in an affluent urban area. But affluent urban women don't generally want to work as nannies. Areas with limited employment opportunities and low wages—like parts of the Midwest and South—are the best places to recruit nannies.

To bridge the gap, nanny services are setting up liaisons with recruiters around the country. Recruiters run ads for nannies in their local papers, then screen respondents. The best candidates are referred to the nanny service, where they are interviewed and, if qualified, placed.

Other potential recruiting grounds are child-care publications, universities and high schools, and the various nanny training schools throughout the country. Most nanny services have basic minimum requirements: high school diploma, child-care experience, driver's license, etc.

Small Start-up, Big Payoff

A nanny placement service can be launched for as little as $11,800. Starting overhead may be kept to a minimum by working from home, or renting a modest single office. This is a "people" business that will depend more on your skills and efficiency than fancy equipment or inventory.

Established nanny placement services are earning healthy profits. On the average, a nanny service that places approximately twelve nannies a month will have annual pre-tax profits of $61,000. This equals about 40 percent of the annual gross sales.

According to a recent study conducted by the Laurel House Press, 71 percent of the 300 nanny services surveyed have been in business for less than five years. And of those businesses surveyed, 44 percent are located in four states. New York has the highest concentration of nanny services,

followed by Massachusetts, Connecticut, and New Jersey.
The majority of the agencies surveyed (72 percent) are doing
business nationwide.

What does this mean? It means there is tremendous opportunity for growth in this industry. Many regions of the
country remain untapped. As more and more mothers enter
the work force, more parents will turn to nanny placement
services to help them find the right child care. And as interest in nanny services increases, the supply of qualified, in-
home child-care providers will no doubt meet the growing
demand.

=========================== BRIGHT IDEA ===========================

SUMMER CAMP GROWS UP

When you were a kid, summer camp was a drag. Now that
you're grown up, does a week in the mountains goofing off
really sound all that bad? The hot news in summer camps is
catering to world-weary adults. Moms flock to a Southern
California mountain resort for a few days of rejuvenation.
Middle-aged sports fans spend thousands to play ball with
ex-major-leaguers.

And then there are the perpetual rockers. At Rock 'n' Roll
Fantasy Camp, San Francisco entrepreneur Gilbert Klein
helps the musically inclined find their place in the spotlight.
Groups of four or five would-be rock stars get together for
intensive week-long jam sessions with accomplished local
musicians. The rock-star hopefuls rehearse, go to rock seminars, and record together before finally performing a free
concert in a San Francisco night club. To commemorate the
experience, campers receive audiotapes of the recording ses-
sion and videos of their rehearsals and concerts.

At $3,500 a pop, you'd almost have to be a rock star to
participate in Klein's camp. Still, for true rock aficionados,
Rock 'n' Roll Fantasy Camp plays like the opportunity of a
lifetime. And besides, says Klein, studio time and a shot at
stardom have never come cheap.

===================== BRIGHT IDEA =====================

SCHOLARSHIP SEARCH

As college tuition continues to skyrocket, more and more students find themselves wishing for scholarships. But according to entrepreneur Mark Cohen, they don't have to wish. "As much as $135 million in scholarships goes unclaimed every year because students don't know which scholarships are out there or how to apply for them," he says.

Cohen, for one, is doing his part to change this. His Academic Guidance Service uses a computer to match students with available scholarships. The Academic Guidance databank is so vast that every student is guaranteed five to twenty-five referrals.

With some research and computer work, it is possible to duplicate Cohen's work. Or you can tap into it via a licensing agreement. For a flat initial fee and a per-use processing charge, licensees gain access to the Academic Guidance computer system. Their work centers on marketing the service, while company headquarters handles the processing.

NAIL SALON

High Net Profit Before Taxes:	$67,000-plus
Average Net Profit Before Taxes:	$46,000
Minimum Start-up:	$20,000
Average Start-up:	$29,000

In the nineties, major excesses may be out, but little indulgences will probably endure. One such luxury is the manicure. In recent years, women have rediscovered the pleasure of getting their nails done. And as a consequence, nail salons have been springing up everywhere.

Start-ups Large and Small

You can start a full-service nail salon with a relatively small investment. Space needs are minimal. Although you should shop around for a convenient location with plenty of foot traffic, you don't need acres of space to set up shop. Simple, attractive furniture and basic equipment and supplies are all you need to open your doors. An average investment of $29,000 will get you started.

If that sounds like a major undertaking to you, consider renting space from an existing beauty salon. You'll help the beauty-shop owner by bringing in new customers and providing an additional service to existing clients. And they'll help you by reducing your rent, furniture, equipment, and marketing costs. By starting out under someone else's roof, you may be able to launch a nail service for less than $10,000. Once your business takes off, you can move to your own location and hire additional operators.

Don't think, however, that the low start-up costs in this business have escaped the notice of other entrepreneurs. In many cities, there are nail salons on every block. Be selective in your choice of locations. A clean, convenient space in a shopping mall, strip center, or business district is a good bet, especially if the neighborhood isn't already swamped with similar operations.

Stress Skill, Marketing

Other competitive factors come into play as well, including skill and marketing. To become a licensed nail technician, you must take courses in chemistry, physiology, aesthetics, sterilization, bacteriology, and a variety of other subjects, usually through a beauty school. Coursework takes about 350 hours, or three and a half months. You must also meet any state or local licensing requirements.

Your skill as a nail technician doesn't depend solely on technical ability. People skills are also a must. Taking the time to learn about your clients' lifestyles, careers, and color preferences will not only enable you to offer better service, but will also help cement customer loyalty.

Of course, outstanding skills won't amount to much if customers never know you exist. Established owners urge newcomers to develop good marketing plans before they get started. Coupon mailers, local newspapers, and cross-promotions with nearby beauty salons are just a few techniques that work. Cultivating referrals is also important: Give free manicures to your friends and ask them to refer their friends and coworkers to your shop.

Experienced nail salon owners stress that this is not a way to get rich quick. Building a solid clientele and expanding the business wisely takes time and commitment. However, this business is accessible to entrepreneurs with limited funds. And with the right combination of professionalism, personality, and perseverance, the nail business does offer excellent earning potential and room for growth.

================= BRIGHT IDEA =================

CLOWNING AROUND

Are you a born clown? Don't despair: Clowning around can be a serious business. For working parents, just keeping the kids fed and clothed is a challenge. Planning and supervising a birthday party is above and beyond the call of duty. If you're a world-class clown, you can command a fairly staggering fee. And you may even turn your clowning into a full-time, on-site venture.

Former actor Jeremy Sage is in greater demand at forty-three than he ever was when he appeared as Jesus in the Broadway production of *Godspell*. The host and main attraction of Jeremy's Place, in Manhattan, magician Sage is booked seven days a week, making him the undisputed king of birthday parties for affluent children in a city where the competition is fierce.

"I've been in this business for twenty-five years, billing myself as 'the worst magician in New York,' " says Sage. "But seven years ago, a number of parents approached me and said they would support a place." So, with money from his acting career, he launched Jeremy's Place in 1982 with the help of his friend Thomas Garbutt, a former set designer.

Garbutt's fantasy designs are part of the magic Jeremy weaves during the ninety-minute performances that cost $600 to $800. That price includes all the traditional party trimmings, Jeremy's bumbling magic act, and a party bag for each guest full of toys and novelties you can't find anywhere else. "Selling party favors is my other business," Sage explains.

========= BRIGHT IDEA =========

APOLOGIES ACCEPTED

Love means never having to say you're sorry—for about 1 percent of the population. The rest of us find apologies part of the regular currency of human relationships. Still, finding the right words (or deeds) to convey your feelings isn't easy. That is, unless you're within calling distance of Los Angeles-based Apologies Accepted.

Company founder Loren Harris dreamed up the idea for customized apologies while watching the movie *Punchline.* In the film, Sally Field apologizes to her husband for spending too many nights at comedy clubs. The scene prompted Harris to think long and hard about the difficulty of apologizing—difficult for the guilty party, that is, but easy for a pro. And who wouldn't spend money to save face?

Harris has created various ways to apologize, say thank you, and express a wide range of human emotions—all with professional pizzazz. Among the stunts: sending floral arrangements, hiring limousines and hot-air balloons, buying theater tickets, and cooking breakfast in bed. Harris and his staff work within three basic parameters: budget, moderate, or deluxe.

INSTANT SHOE-REPAIR SHOP

High Net Profit Before Taxes:	$114,000
Average Net Profit Before Taxes:	$47,500
Minimum Start-up:	$55,000
Average Start-up:	$95,000

Shoe shoppers around the country are experiencing a new sensation: sticker shock. A good pair of pumps can cost upwards of $100 and a pair of men's dress shoes can weigh in at $150 or more. Prices like these could prompt consumers to go barefoot—or at least give their old shoes a second look.

Shoe repair is an old industry that's taking on a new face. Traditional shoe-repair shops continue to prosper, but so do a new breed of instant shoe-repair services that give new meaning to the term "walk-in service."

Instant shoe-repair shops exist primarily in malls and other busy shopping districts. Their specialty: fast turn-around. Simple jobs take as little as fifteen or twenty minutes, so customers can literally walk in and walk out with a renewed pair of shoes.

The real emphasis is on convenience. In surveys, consumers revealed that they felt shoe repair was the personal service least appropriately offered. On the whole, people did not know where to go for shoe repair, considered existing locations obscure, and indicated a need for more convenient locations. Of course, this hasn't prevented 43 percent of the population from getting its shoes fixed. For all its problems, shoe repair represents a $1 billion industry, according to the Baltimore-based Shoe Service Institute of America. If shoe-repair services can offer consumers a more convenient alternative, the market should experience healthy growth.

A "Shoe-In" for Success

Skeptics might wonder whether a shoe-repair business can survive in the high-rent world of shopping malls. The answer, according to people in the business, is a resounding yes. One reason is that instant shoe-repair shops require little space: 300 to 600 square feet is usually sufficient. The other reason, of course, is sales.

"One instant shoe-repair chain has the highest average sales per square foot ($1,200 per square foot) of any franchise operation in the world," said one industry expert. "The average annual gross sales exceeds $250,000." The stores' sales volume ranges from $125,000 to $550,000. Independent operations can expect similar income, with pretax net profits in the $50,000 to $100,000 range.

What makes instant shoe repair so lucrative? According

to one owner we consulted, the difference is accessibility. "We are an impulse retailer," he explains. "Our sales are not always a planned trip. Thirty percent of our business is someone who left home in the morning and had no idea they were going to have their shoes repaired that day." For that reason, it is possible for an instant shoe-repair business to coexist profitably near a traditional shoe repair shop—sometimes even within the same city block. Instant shoe repair appeals largely to those who wouldn't normally repair their shoes. And that includes over half the population.

Thanks to Technology

Anyone who has had their shoes repaired knows it takes two or three days to get them fixed. Then how can an instant shoe-repair shop rebuild a pair of shoes in fifteen to twenty minutes?

Instant shoe repair stresses expediency over craftsmanship. A traditional shop will glue the sole of a shoe, tap it down, then wait for the glue to dry under a heat lamp—a process that takes hours. Instant shops use glue that takes twenty seconds to dry. The shoe is placed under a hydraulic press with a couple thousand pounds per square inch of pressure. Afterwards, the sole will be bonded to the shoe much like the original manufacturing process.

Traditionalists don't put much stock in the quality of instant repairs. But instant shoe-repair entrepreneurs (and apparently the buying public) maintain that the quality is fine—and a fast, convenient repair is better than none at all.

This argument between traditionalists and instant repairers raises a dilemma for the aspiring entrepreneur. In order to start a successful shop, you will probably have to learn instant shoe repair yourself and/or be willing to train a staff. Experienced shoe-repair people probably won't have the kind of background you need. Training your own staff can be a good investment, however. Once the business is established, you may be able to operate it as an absentee owner.

SAVING SOLES

Bruce Baker, president of Heels on Wheels, a mobile shoe-shine and shoe-repair franchise, was attending theology school in Dallas when he had a startling revelation. "While walking through a Dallas-area mall, I noticed the long lines in front of a number of shoeshine booths," he says, "so I decided a shoeshine booth might be a good way to subsidize my job in the ministry."

In June 1984, Baker graduated and returned home to Phoenix, where he promptly built a two-seated, oak shoe-shine booth. He placed the booth in a medium-sized Phoenix-area mall, in which he was given a prime location near the entrance of the mall.

Baker remained at that location for a year, until a restaurant agreed to lease the space. Though Baker was given a new location in the mall, he found it less lucrative.

Many of his customers had been asking him about a mobile shoeshine service. Now that he had lost his location, Baker decided the time was right to go ahead with the idea.

Baker threw his shoeshine equipment in the trunk of his car and started visiting some of his regular clients in late 1985. In the beginning, Baker averaged fifty clients a week, both at home and at their businesses. By June 1986, through cold calling businesses and homes, Baker was averaging 1,000 clients a week. "The rapid growth necessitated a van," he says. "Pulling the equipment out of the trunk at each stop took up too much time."

As his clientele grew, Baker decided to expand his services. Along with the shoeshines, he wanted to offer shoe repairs. He eventually found a man to teach him the art of shoe repair. Every Saturday, Baker went to this man's shop, where he practiced repairing the heels and soles of old shoes.

When Baker had mastered the new craft in late 1986, he furnished his van with the necessary equipment and began offering the new service to his clients. "For a while, I only repaired heels out of the van," he explains. "I sent all the sole work back to the shop as a thanks for the help."

========================= BRIGHT IDEA =========================

MAKING ROOM FOR BABY

When Kathy Stephens set out to furnish her first child's nursery, she was so dissatisfied with the decor available on the market that she started redecorating from scratch. Shortly thereafter, requests started pouring in from friends.

"After doing my own nursery, I did so many decorating jobs for friends that I decided I could do children's interior design for a living," Stephens says. And she was right. Just five years after she decorated her first nursery, Stephens began franchising her Phoenix, Arizona-based children's design service, Childscapes. Already, the company has four branches in Arizona and plans to expand nationwide.

Busy working parents are an ideal market for children's design, but according to Stephens there is also room in the commercial market for resourceful designers. She maintains that a formal design background is not as important as good sense and style. "We look for [franchisees] with a knowledge of children and a flair for art and creativity," she says.

========================= BRIGHT IDEA =========================

STAKING YOUR CLAIM

Across the country, people are experiencing a terminal condition: form-a-phobia. They hate insurance forms. They hate loan forms. They hate tax forms. In fact, when it comes down to it, most people hate any kind of form that's more than three lines long. It's not that they take three hours to complete (which they often do). It's that they require the reasoning skills of Pascal and the patience of Mother Teresa.

But filling out forms isn't tedious for the staff at Med-I-Claims Services Inc., a Peoria, Illinois-based company with licensees across the country. Med-I-Claims specializes in completing and submitting medical forms to insurance companies for people who hate to do it themselves.

Company president Joan Kirkpatrick, whose late husband Richard launched the company in 1984, reports that Med-I-Claims fills a great need in today's graying society. "Some of our clients are bedridden, or too ill to fill out insurance forms," she explains. "But without the forms, they can't receive the benefits. To them, our service is very valuable."

Consumers seem to think so, too. Med-I-Claims has six locations including licensees, and is hoping to expand nationwide.

BUSINESS SERVICES

TEMPORARY HELP SERVICE

High Net Profit Before Taxes:	$220,000
Average Net Profit Before Taxes:	$45,000
Minimum Start-up:	$15,000
Average Start-up:	$35,000

Call it fear of commitment. Employers no longer want to hire full-time employees that they may not be able to support forever. In truth, many projects don't require a permanent employee—just a temporary boost in staff. The accounting department needs help closing the books. The marketing department wants their figures put into a database. The receptionist is going on vacation for three weeks.

What works for employers also works for a growing number of temporary workers. Americans are mobile these days. When a couple relocates to a new city so one can accept a new job, the other may work at a temporary agency until something permanent comes along. Other temporary workers never want a permanent position: They enjoy the flexibility of being a "temp," working only the days and hours they prefer. The lifestyle is so appealing, in fact, that temporary work is no longer limited to clerical duties. Today's "Kelly girl" is likely to be a doctor, executive, graphic artist, lawyer, or nurse.

These dual trends add up to the third fastest-growing

industry in the United States, according to the National Association of Temporary Services. Today, nine out of ten businesses use temporary help at some time. There are more than 2,000 temporary help services in this country. And though established franchises do exist, many successful temporary help services are independently owned and operated.

Don't Call It an Agency

A temporary help service is not an employment agency. A traditional employment agency matches unemployed workers with jobs, acting as a kind of broker. A temporary help service is the employer. The service screens, interviews, and hires workers who are then sent out to various client worksites. The temporary help service pays that worker his or her wages, as well as any applicable taxes and benefits. In turn, the service collects an hourly fee from the client. Thus, the temporary help service isn't an agency, but a business service.

The temporary help service makes its money on markup. If the going hourly rate for a data-entry clerk in your area is $10, and a nearby company needs one for a day or a week, you'd charge the company $15 to $18 an hour to deliver on the spot. The difference is your "take," or gross profit.

Why would a business pay $18 an hour for someone it could hire itself for $10? Because you save that business time. If the business had to interview, test, and train an employee itself, it could waste hundreds of dollars' worth of time. That's the secret to profitability in this business. And that's why temporary help services are closing in on a $6 billion annual market.

A Changing Image

Years ago, temporary help meant unskilled day labor or someone who could do passable typing and envelope-stuffing. Business owners brought them in to do "grunt work" at low pay. But today, temporary help services emphasize professionalism and specialization—and they deliver on both counts.

Most temporary help services are generalists. They can provide the right worker for almost any function—from light clerical and typing tasks to manning a trade-show booth or operating a ten-key adding machine.

But the fastest-growing segment of the market with the highest profit potential is in specialty temporary services. If your market is big enough to support an operation that delivers only data-processing specialists, legal secretaries, or accounting professionals, you may have a lucrative niche to fill. Because specialized skills are more difficult to find, technical and professional jobs command higher hourly or daily rates—and higher markups as well.

If you're unsure of the specialty market in your area, consider adopting a focus. Run ads focusing on specific categories of workers in different sections of the Yellow Pages or newspaper. This way, you can give the impression of having a specialty while maintaining the volume potential of a general service.

Be Versatile

A temporary help service undergoes a variety of functions throughout the average business day. A typical day might include interviewing applicants, testing candidates, pitching clients, solving problems, handling payroll, taking orders, and making assignments.

Several skills are necessary in this business. First, you must be a hiring expert. Clients are willing to pay extra for your employees, but only if they're skilled and qualified. Therefore, it's essential that you develop a testing and interviewing process that gives you an accurate picture of a worker's abilities. At the same time, you must also find a way to elicit specific information from clients on the kinds of skills they require. Only then can you make an agreeable match.

Second, you must be able to market your services. Few cities are without established temporary help services. In order to thrive, you must have a workable plan. Know who your potential clients are and how you're going to reach them before you launch your service. Once you're up and running, don't let up on your marketing efforts.

Third, you must be an administrative whiz. Your employees are going to visit several job sites. They are going to have varying hours at varying salaries. Each is going to have to have a host of deductions taken from each paycheck. Meanwhile, every employer is different. You have to know whom to bill, how much to charge, and when their payment is due.

These are just a few of the skills you'll need to run a temporary help service. Of course, you don't have to excel in all areas. If you need help, you can hire a manager, accountant, or salesperson. But remember that this isn't a simple business. On one hand, you don't have inventory hassles or high retail rent to contend with. But on the flip side, you will rely more heavily on your ability to manage the business and to do a good job.

===================== BRIGHT IDEA =====================

NURSES ON CALL

The shortage of qualified nurses in America is fast becoming a crisis situation for hospitals and patients alike. However, an innovative temporary-help service called TravCorps Corp. is stepping in to lend a helping hand.

Company president Bruce Male explains that his Malden, Massachusetts-based firm provides hospitals with temporary nurses who travel all over the country, working for a period of one to three months. The nurses' costs are covered by TravCorps, and the payment schedule is arranged according to the specifications of the hospital. "The hospital can put the nurses on their payroll, or they can pay us and have us pay the nurses," says Male.

Male believes the profit potential for his business and others like it is unlimited. And the concept TravCorps pioneered is catching on fast, he adds, saying, "Since we started the business, we've been joined by about sixty competitors."

PAYROLL PROCESSING

People start their own businesses for all kinds of reasons, but one of them usually isn't a love of payrolls. For the average businessperson, payroll processing is an ongoing nightmare. Unless, of course, that person is in the business of payroll processing.

If you have basic bookkeeping and accounting skills and are computer literate, you may have what it takes to start your own payroll company. Here's a basic rundown of services payroll processing companies provide:

- Departmental payroll registers
- Departmental general ledgers
- Employee W-2 forms
- Employee status changes, such as new hires and layoffs
- Check registers
- Earnings stubs
- Employee year-to-date earnings
- Payroll checks
- Employer payroll tax summaries
- Employee master listing
- Vacation and sick-time summaries
- Worker's compensation summaries

It's easy to see how these tasks can overwhelm the average entrepreneur. Even larger companies sometimes prefer the convenience and efficiency of farming out their payrolls. Yet for the payroll specialist, keeping track of checks, tax requirements, and government regulations are all in a day's work.

"[Unlike a company accountant], we don't get sick, go on vacation, or leave the firm," says B. Thomas Golisano, founder, chairman, and CEO of Paychex Inc., a Rochester, New York-based payroll processing firm with eighty-four offices nationwide. "With payroll tax rules in a constant state of flux and delinquency, and fines running as high as $300 for every day a $3,000 tax payment is late, [our service allows] the business owner to rest easy, knowing that we will deliver his or her reports and payments on schedule."

To start a payroll-processing business, you need basic accounting skills and knowledge of tax laws and regulations. You also need to develop a computerized system for generating payroll (at an average charge of $1.50 per paycheck, you have to work fast). You do not, however, need an expensive office or an expansive staff in the beginning. Concentrate on building a solid client base and expanding your services gradually.

COUPON MAILING SERVICE

High Net Profit Before Taxes:	$75,000
Average Net Profit Before Taxes:	$50,000
Minimum Start-up:	$4,000
Average Start-up:	$7,000

Advertising is expensive. For large companies with multi-million-dollar budgets, advertising effectively is difficult enough. But for small local businesses, the problem can be nearly impossible to solve.

Newspaper and electronic media ads are common choices, but they often aren't the most effective. Advertisers pay to reach a wide range of people, many of whom aren't likely prospects. Direct mail can be a more accurate alternative, but is also expensive. Between printing, postage, and labor costs, a direct-mail campaign can cost more than it brings in.

Co-op mailing programs offer the effectiveness of direct mail at a lower cost. In a co-op mailing, goods or services from more than one company are promoted via coupons or reply cards sent in the same envelope. Advertisers share space and mailing expense cooperatively.

The Co-op Concept

Perhaps you've received co-op mailers yourself. The R.H. Donnelly/Carol Wright Co-Op goes out to more than 18 million homes several times a year. Each mailing contains a variety of slick cents-off coupons for nationally advertised products; sometimes it also includes product samples.

You can provide a similar service locally. As a co-op mailer, you can offer local merchants and small-business owners the opportunity to zero in on prospects close to their places of business. Because your mailing will be relatively small, the cost of participating in your program will be low.

Direct mail marketing has become so sophisticated that it's possible to target just about any group of people your clients want. So, for instance, you can coordinate a mailing to every household in your zip code. If your clients are upscale, you might select just households with incomes over $50,000. You can target credit-card holders, business owners, mail-order buyers, singles, families with children—the list of factors you can specify goes on and on. The key is matching the right clients with their appropriate markets.

Double-Edged Market

First, put together a mailing list. There are co-op delivery services being created for many markets: college, home, business-and-professional, hobby, recreational, male, female, teen, religious, scholarly, and many more. You may also select your list by geographical location—a boon to local retailers, for example. Plenty of unsaturated markets are up for grabs. You can create low-cost direct-mail campaigns to reach any or all of them. For more information on existing mailing lists available for rent, contact a mailing list broker or the Standard Rate and Data Service catalogs in your local library.

Once you've established whom you're going to reach, contact businesses that cater to your clientele. For instance, if your list includes local working singles, you might contact dating services, health clubs, restaurants, pizza delivery services, hair and nail salons, cleaning services, and bars.

Spend a few hours scanning a mailing-list directory. Markets you never dreamed of will suddenly become amazingly accessible, and trade advertisements in the directory will provide first-rate information free. When you're ready to put your list together, contact a mailing list broker. He or she will help you secure the lists you want, usually at no additional cost to you.

====================== BRIGHT IDEA ======================

A FAX IN YOUR FUTURE?

Some entrepreneurs want to do it all; others want just the fax. In recent years, the fax has become an indispensable tool for doing business, yet not every business can justify the expense of buying its own.

Thus, many businesses use fax services. For a per-page fee, they can send or receive faxed documents without the cost of buying a machine. Most fax services are located within other businesses—print and copy shops, convenience stores, office supply shops, and so on. If you don't have an existing operation in which to set up, consider starting a fax service at someone else's location.

Fax-9, a national franchise based in Colorado Springs, Colorado, has 167 sites in forty-two states and Canada. The host location's employees operate the fax service. "We complement various retail and service operations, including banks, travel agencies, photo shops, typesetters, post offices, drugstores, and courthouse coffee shops," says Rene Boutin, president of Fax-9.

According to Susan Jacquelin, owner of Trade Wind Printing in Honolulu, Hawaii, having Fax-9 in the shop has really boosted business. "The Fax-9 service offers an added value for our customers," she says. "After just four months, Fax-9 has definitely improved the foot traffic in our store. So many customers say, 'How did we do business without them?'"

ActionFax, another franchised fax service, reports similar success in print and copy shops, convenience stores, building lobbies, airports, and hotels. "Heavy foot traffic and street visibility are two key ingredients to success," says Steven Gordon, national marketing manager for the company. Estimated start-up costs for an ActionFax franchised fax booth are about $2,700, including all of the necessary equipment and a franchise fee of about $500.

APARTMENT-PREPARATION SERVICE

High Net Profit Before Taxes:	$65,000
Average Net Profit Before Taxes:	$16,000
Minimum Start-up:	$2,000
Average Start-up:	$6,500

These days, Americans are mobile. Some 53 percent of the population rents property. In any given year, a hefty percentage of units in any apartment complex will turn over. When tenants leave, units are rarely ready to show. Cleaning, painting, and minor repairs are standard. Yet many landlords don't have the time (or the inclination) to handle these tasks. When this is the case, many turn to professional apartment-preparation services.

With an unusually low investment and no special training, you can tap into this vast market. Apartment-preparation services typically offer anything from a good housecleaning to complete restoration. An average overhaul, including carpet-cleaning, painting, window-washing, and minor touch-ups takes less than 48 hours. The average fee? Between $250 and $600.

One operator we contacted started with less than $1,000 in operating capital and saw $50,000 his first year. Some established apartment-maintenance companies employ crews of people and pull in more than $75,000 a year.

Marketing's the Trick

The elements of an apartment-preparation service are simple. Just about anyone can learn to clean, paint, and perform minor repairs. For more complicated work, you can contract with other businesses—drapery cleaners, for example. What separates successful services from their less successful counterparts is marketing. You'll need hardy salesmanship and professional follow-through to make money in this business. Practical knowledge accounts for only 10 percent of your job. The other 90 percent is good, solid marketing.

Your potential customers will include property management companies, realty companies, and independent land-lords. Building contractors frequently require final cleanup after a new housing project, apartment complex, or condo development has been completed so that new tenants can take possession with a minimum of fuss. This represents another potential market for your services.

Think of yourself as a convenience store for property owners. Chances are, other vendors already supply the services you'll offer. But most of these work independently. To enlist their services, a landlord would have to make three or four phone calls and sign as many contracts, thereby wasting his or her valuable time. Property owners are busy people. Deadlines can be tight, and most jobs will fall into the "rush" category. As long as you're equipped to handle the demand, this dynamic works to your advantage. Your one-stop service is clearly the fastest, most efficient way for the property owner to go.

===================== BRIGHT IDEA =====================

LEGAL-EASE

The laws of supply and demand say that low supply brings high demand. And in this world where the public is fast to rectify their problems through litigation, the supply of legal support personnel is extremely low. Louise Hackett, founder of Legalstaff Inc., a franchise based in Sacramento, California, has recognized that demand and is capitalizing on it with her own law-office placement firm.

As a legislative aide with the California State Senate sixteen years ago, Hackett sought the services of a legal employment agency only to find that one didn't exist. In an effort to remedy the problem, she started Legal Personnel Services, a full-service legal placement company, in 1973. Today, Hackett's business has grown into a multi-million-dollar company with one office in Sacramento, one in San Francisco, and a third in Mountain View, California.

As a natural progression from owning and operating her own business, Hackett expanded her legal personnel concept by creating Legalstaff Inc. in 1987, in order to franchise her concept. Franchising has also enabled Hackett to expand her business without feeling too overextended. It freed her to open more offices without having to worry about running them all herself.

Starting an employment agency for legal workers isn't so different from starting a regular employment agency. Finding qualified workers, meeting client demands, and using smart marketing strategies are the central elements in both businesses. But having a specialty gives Legalstaff added credibility in a field that demands high standards—and needs plenty of qualified help.

COLLECTION AGENCY

High Net Profit Before Taxes:	$240,000
Average Net Profit Before Taxes:	$50,000
Minimum Start-up:	$9,400
Average Start-up:	$15,000

Looking for a good way to pay your bills? Start a business that makes other people pay theirs. Collection agencies are thriving in small towns and major cities alike, many of them grossing six- and seven-figure annual incomes.

One operation we investigated started five years ago on an investment of $750 and is now a multi-office service netting its husband-and-wife owners more than $150,000 annually. Typically, pretax nets are in the 25- to 35-percent range.

Give Us Some Credit

Much of America is running on credit. The national debt has doubled in the last five years, exceeding $2 trillion today. Americans owe more than $1 trillion on housing alone.

In addition, we owe more than $547.7 billion in installment debt. This doesn't include doctor and dentist bills; money owed to accountants, attorneys, or hospitals; or any credit card amount that's paid off in less than thirty days. Plastic credit cards—more than 600 million of them, or 3.2 for every adult in the country—are helping fuel the fire. In fact, many Americans use up to twenty-three cents of every take-home dollar just to pay off their debts. Today, there are more than 2.5 million institutions that grant credit, so it's no wonder that the credit and collections business is booming.

Basics of the Business

How does a collection agency work? Agencies act on behalf of creditors who have been unable to collect payment for products or services rendered. The agency collects the amount due from the client's customers, and charges a commission on the amount collected. Typical commissions are 25 percent on the first $1,000, 30 to 50 percent on accounts under $50, and a $25 minimum charge on accounts from $50 to $125.

A collection agency's clients include just about any business that grants credit—retailers, doctors, dentists, hospitals, service businesses, manufacturers, and so on. Oil companies that issue credit cards are another market prospect, as are utility companies.

In most areas, collection agencies already exist. But this doesn't mean you can't attract your share of accounts. Collection agencies thrive on competition. Many clients like to divide their accounts between several agencies, hoping that this spirit of competition will help retrieve receivables.

Usually, there is enough business to go around. We investigated seven agencies in a town of 300,000 people and discovered that all the agencies were making a profit. The lowest, a one-man operation, was bringing in a 15-percent pretax net, and the largest, with a staff of ten, was bringing in pretax net profits of $200,000, or 28 percent.

Experience Counts

Starting a collection agency does not require a large capital investment. Since most of your work is done over the phone or by correspondence, you don't need a fancy location. Many successful firms were launched from home with little more than a desk, telephone, stationery, and marketing plan. You may even start the business on a part-time basis while you hold down your current job.

You will need some expertise, however. The collection business is highly regulated and, in most cities, highly competitive. Though some entrepreneurs have made money in this field with little prior experience, you have a far better chance of succeeding if you learn the business before you start. The best place to start is probably on the job. Working for another collection agency—even for a short time—will give you invaluable training.

===== BRIGHT IDEA =====

OFFICE ORGANIZING

Organization is a skill every businessperson should have. But unfortunately, many don't. Unfortunately, that is, for everyone but the growing number of professional office organizers.

Office organizers do everything from setting up files to clearing off desks. Typical duties include buying the right furniture and equipment (and throwing out ill-chosen items), creating a workable bookkeeping system, and teaching clients the finer points of time management. For this, you do not need much formal training. What you do need is a clear head and a flair for setting things straight.

You can start an office organizing service from your home with little more than business stationery, transportation, and a working phone. Executives, entrepreneurs, doctors, dentists, and other professionals are your main market— although one office organizer we spoke with reported a healthy market in organizing garages, kitchens, and home offices as well.

CONSULTING BUSINESS

High Net Profit Before Taxes:	$70,000-plus
Average Net Profit Before Taxes:	$42,000
Minimum Start-up:	$8,000
Average Start-up:	$18,000

If you're an expert in a specific field of business, your advice could be worth $100 an hour or more. Depending on your area of expertise, you could gross between $175 to $900 per day as an independent business consultant.

Do these fees sound steep to you? Then consider the cost of hiring a permanent full-time technical advisor, executive, or other specialist. Conversely, consider the cost of going without much-needed information. For many small businesses, government agencies, and individuals, hiring a consultant is the only way to get the help they need on a budget.

Many people claim they could never be consultants because they don't have enough experience or knowledge. But the fact is that most people don't realize how much they really know, or how specialized their knowledge is. Of course, not everyone can be a successful consultant—you do need some experience and information. But if you have specialized knowledge about marketing, technology, finance, business planning, or even a more offbeat area of business, you may have the starting material for a consulting business of your own.

A Wide Range of Options

When most of us think of consultants, we envision retired government officials or top corporate executives lending their expertise for big bucks. However, today's consultants run the gamut from ex-executives to entrepreneurs, health-care specialists, and teachers.

Our research uncovered professional consultants who coordinate and run garage sales for clients. Two women in New York City run a consulting business rearranging furniture in homes or office to create a new look. Their experience? Rearranging the furniture in their own homes over the years. These are classic examples of how you can turn an unusual skill or specialty into a business—even without an impressive string of degrees or years of training. If you do have numerous degrees and years of training, all the better. Your specialty may be readymade.

To give you a sample of the diversity of the consulting industry, here are just a few of the consulting businesses we uncovered during the course of our research: home decorat-

ing, wedding planning, library consulting, astrology, dealing
with death, time management, wardrobe planning, career
planning, health maintenance, storage organization, mem-
ory development, defensive driving, party consulting, pet
consulting, cooking, shopping consulting, speech consulting, retirement counseling, and shyness counseling.

To choose your best field, take stock of your background
and interests. What do you know most about? What do you
have a knack for? What do you enjoy doing? And, perhaps
most important, what would clients pay money to have you
do? Remember that the three main benefits of any consulting service are 1) to save the client time, 2) to save the
client money, and 3) to provide the client with information.
Keep these criteria in mind when zeroing in on the right
field. Your services must be marketable in order to fly.

Identify Your Markets

The two basic markets for consulting services are the
private sector and the public sector. In many fields of business consulting, it's possible to serve both these markets.

The government is a major purchaser of consulting services, spending billions of dollars a year on advice. In addition to hiring consultants directly, the government also
creates work for consultants through private-sector contracts. When an organization wins a government contract, it
may require the help of consultants in several fields. It may
have been given funds to complete a specific task within a
certain time, and may need temporary technical aid, political
liaison, or specific skills to accomplish that task. Also, in
order to obtain the government contract, a company might
bring in consultants in other fields to improve its organization so it will gain government acceptance.

The private sector is also a goldmine of opportunity for
the independent consultant. The same employment trends
that make temporary help services popular apply to consultants. Many employers need immediate help with specific
problems. Rather than hiring a full-time employee, many opt
to take on part-time or temporary consultants. Whether your
expertise is in turning failing companies around or raising
capital for expansion, your services are probably in demand.

Before you launch your consulting business, try to home in on your target market. Will you be catering to small, one-person firms? Large corporations? Your city government? Individuals? Do you want to restrict your market to local firms, or are you willing to travel? Many consultants start out by using contacts established on the job. Do you currently have any contacts that might help you launch your new business?

Whatever your target market, be sure to map out a marketing plan before you start the business. In general, consultants bill an average of only fourteen working days per month directly to their clients. The rest of their time is spent marketing. The more efficient your marketing operations are, the more time you will have to devote to billable hours—and the better your chances of having clients to bill.

========= BRIGHT IDEA =========

PACKING THEM IN

Around the country, businesses and consumers alike are bringing their sendables to independent services for packing and shipping. But you don't need an independent location to launch this type of service. Packy The Shipper, a Racine, Wisconsin-based franchise, has found a niche for itself in office supply and gift shops.

"Packy The Shipper franchisees have also been successful in drugstores, convenience stores, and hardware stores," notes Arnold Johnson, vice president of operations. "Frankly, this is not intended as a high-volume business or a stand-alone parcel and packing store. The whole idea is to offer an additional service and get additional customers into your store."

Locating within an existing shop is the key to viability in this business. "If you were to operate [a packing and shipping service] on your own, you would have to pay rent, wages, insurance, taxes, and so forth. But when it's run as an add-on service [to an existing business], all that is taken care of."

Packy The Shipper has approximately 1,500 operators

nationwide. The franchisees pay $395 or less for the use of a state-of-the-art electronic digital scale, plus all the necessary marketing tools, including signs, handbills, and point-of-purchase displays. A typical location ships fifteen to thirty-five packages per week, yielding gross revenues of $4,000 to $9,000 annually, a tidy supplement to a shopowner's income. But this concept isn't limited to established entrepreneurs. Aspiring businesspeople might consider setting up similar operations within other people's stores.

MOBILE BOOKKEEPING SERVICE

High Net Profit Before Taxes:	$60,000
Average Net Profit Before Taxes:	$40,000
Minimum Start-up:	$25,000
Average Start-up:	$45,000

Mobile bookkeepers have given a new twist to an old business. By providing small-business owners with a bookkeeping service that is faster, cheaper, and more convenient, mobile bookkeepers are stealing the small-business market from their office-bound counterparts.

Traditional bookkeepers perform their services in offices and usually require two to three weeks to complete the work, and another week to meet with the owner and discuss his or her financial position. Meanwhile, the business owners are without their books and financial data, hindering their ability to conduct business.

The mobile bookkeeper eliminates these problems. By equipping vans with all the amenities of an office, the mobile bookkeeper can arrive at the business, complete the books, print the reports, and discuss them with the owner all in a matter of hours. And because the financial information never leaves the parking lot, the business is not inconvenienced.

Mobile bookkeeping became possible with the introduction of the personal computer, which is small enough to transport easily and powerful enough to perform the necessary bookkeeping functions.

This industry is still young, but is expected to expand rapidly over the next ten years. The growth of mobile bookkeeping will be linked with the growth of small and medium-sized businesses, which are the prime market for mobile bookkeepers. Smaller companies generally can't afford their own in-house accountants.

Overall, mobile bookkeeping services target companies with fewer than twenty employees. According to the Bureau of Government Statistics, 83 percent of all businesses in America have the necessary population to support a mobile bookkeeping service. Many mobile bookkeepers suggest locating in areas with a population of at least 60,000. Look at both the population of the area and the number of small businesses operating within it when deciding on a location. Most operators recommend that an area have a population of at least 50,000 and within that, at least 5,000 businesses with twenty employees or less.

Attracting Customers

The success of a mobile bookkeeping service depends on the strength of the operator's accounting and bookkeeping background. Although you don't have to be a CPA to run a mobile bookkeeping service, it is best to have extensive accounting and bookkeeping experience.

However, it is possible to run a successful operation even if you have no accounting or bookkeeping experience. You can simply hire the qualified accountants to do the actual bookkeeping. These accountants are usually paid a percentage of their gross billings. A commissioned, open-ended salary provides an incentive to do the work quickly and efficiently.

In addition to hiring a staff with the requisite bookkeeping skills, a mobile bookkeeping service must have a vehicle large enough to provide sufficient work space, but small enough to be operated efficiently. Most services use commercial-sized vans at least 21 feet in length with 87 square feet of internal area.

A large cabinet on one side of the van houses all of the equipment during travel and folds down into a desk for working. Other cabinets can hold equipment such as a personal computer and printer, a copy machine, a calculator, business forms, computer paper, and miscellaneous office supplies. Additionally, there should be two chairs so that meetings with clients can be held in the privacy of the van.

Most mobile bookkeeping vans can service between four and five clients a day, depending on the client's size and business activity.

To acquire a solid client base, mobile bookkeepers rely on a variety of advertising and marketing strategies. The local Yellow Pages are the most popular advertising medium for mobile bookkeepers. Some mobile bookkeepers also advertise in business journals and on radio stations. They contend that these types of advertising provide good public relations, even if they do not bring in business directly.

The mobile bookkeeping van itself also provides plenty of free advertising, since the company name and telephone number are painted on the side.

Advertising aside, most bookkeepers agree that cold calling and canvassing are the most effective methods of marketing. "I have one salesperson working for me," says one successful operator. "He calls on businesses and passes out brochures that explain our services. We get 90 percent of our business this way."

A Look in the Book

When a new client is enlisted, there is often a considerable amount of back work to be completed before the monthly service can begin. Because most owners of small businesses are not accountants, they neglect their books. So when they do hire a bookkeeper, the books are usually months behind.

"When we pick up a new client, chances are they haven't done anything for the year," says one mobile bookkeeping franchisee. "So we have to bring their books up to date."

Back work usually entails doing several months of bookkeeping in a few hours. Many bookkeeping services charge extra for this, unless the books need only minor adjustments.

From looking at the back work, an accountant can usually get some idea of how much to charge for the monthly service. Most mobile bookkeepers charge a flat fee based on the client's business activity, which includes the number of employees, the number of checks written, and the number of bank accounts. The average minimum monthly fee is about $75.

Once the fees are established, clients are given a list of expense accounts and told which items pertain to each expense category. Then they are encouraged to code all check stubs as the checks are written. This speeds up future bookkeeping.

After the client has been trained to code checks correctly, the actual monthly service can begin. Once a month, the mobile bookkeeping service arrives at the business site to begin work.

The bookkeeper starts by making adjustments to the previous month's books. Next, the accountant reconciles bank statements. Check stubs are verified with the bank statements, and any checks that have not cleared are subtracted from the total. Check stubs are then input into the computer, and reports are generated.

Standard bookkeeping reports include income/loss statements, balance sheets, receipts reports, and payroll reports unique to their businesses.

When the reports have been generated, the accountant sits down with the client to review them. This is an important part of the service because most small-business owners have neither the time nor the accounting knowledge to make sense of the reports on their own.

Getting Started

The start-up costs for a mobile bookkeeping service are relatively low. The cost of a van and its modifications is the largest expenditure, ranging from $30,000 to $50,000, which includes all the computer and office equipment.

Another attractive feature of a mobile bookkeeping service is the low overhead. Gas for the van, computer paper, and office supplies constitute most of the overhead.

Mobile bookkeeping is a young industry with plenty of growth potential. Entrepreneurs who have already begun mobile bookkeeping services are enjoying the rewards of entering an industry on the ground floor.

RÉSUMÉ WRITING AND CAREER COUNSELING

High Net Profit Before Taxes:	$33,000
Average Net Profit Before Taxes:	$27,000
Minimum Start-up:	$3,000
Average Start-up:	$12,000

It's a fact as certain as death and taxes: Everyone looks for a job at least once. And when they do, most need résumés. A good résumé can spell the difference between getting an interview and getting overlooked, yet most people don't know the first thing about selling themselves on paper.

This doesn't apply only to blue-collar workers and recent college graduates, either. Mergers, acquisitions, restructuring, and downsizing have left plenty of people looking for work. Engineers, accountants, middle managers, and other professionals need help, too. Summarizing twenty years of work experience on a single page is no small feat. In fact, some people find that simply typing a résumé is a stress-inducing task.

In today's society, we're accustomed to getting outside help. How many of us do our own taxes, fix our own cars, or remodel our own homes? At work, the trend is equally evident. Consultants, advisors, and temporary support staff are all permanent fixtures in the modern workplace. So is it any wonder that out-of-work professionals seek professional help with their résumés?

What Goes In

Résumé-writing services vary in scope and size. Some concentrate on production: Clients write their own copy and hand it over to the service for typesetting and printing. This service is a good add-on to a typesetting or printing shop. Other operations offer a full range of services, from writing and editing the résumé to typing, layout, printing, and mailing. A full-service résumé firm may also provide career counseling or seminars on interviewing, cold calling, and negotiation.

You do not need any particular experience to start a résumé-writing service, although you should have some talent for the services you offer. For instance, if you plan to write copy for your clients, you should be reasonably adept at producing clear, concise, intelligent writing. If you plan to stress layout, you should have some background in graphics. Of course, the important thing is not your experience, but your results. Can you produce a good résumé? If so, you have the beginnings of a viable service.

Remember, though, that a good full-service résumé firm does more than slap words down on paper. To establish a solid reputation (and therefore referrals), you'll need to maintain strict standards of quality, service, honesty, and reliability.

Equip Yourself

To produce professional-quality résumés, you'll need access to the following equipment: a computer with word-processing or desktop-publishing capabilities, a laser printer, a filing system, a printing press and/or copy machines. You do not have to buy all of this equipment up front. If your finances are tight, consider leasing some of the equipment, or using outside services to provide what you can't afford (for instance, you can send printing work to an instant print shop).

Your facility does not have to be posh, just presentable. Your space requirements will depend on the amount of equipment you purchase, but most résumé-writing services are run out of small offices. Look for a space that will accommodate your work area and a small reception area where you can meet with clients. It is possible to launch a résumé-writing service from home by offering pick-up and delivery services, but an outside office will enable clients to drop by without feeling awkward.

Getting Clients

As in any business, the success of a résumé-writing service depends on good marketing and promotion. Start with a basic ad in the Yellow Pages, but don't stop there. Look for unusual places to advertise—job journals are a natural outlet, and college newspapers are often good for reaching the younger crowd.

One of the largest markets available to résumé-writing firms is the corporate market. When a company lays workers off, it runs the risk of being sued for wrongful termination, and it incurs a fair amount of negative publicity. Hiring a career-counseling service to help displaced workers is a smart gesture of goodwill, and many companies are willing to shoulder the cost.

This business lends itself well to attracting publicity. Make yourself a local expert on job hunting: Read up on the latest job-search techniques and hiring trends. Call your local paper and offer to do a story on how to write an effective résumé, or send a press release that identifies the ten most common mistakes people make when putting their résumés together.

In a similar vein, consider teaching a course on job-hunting at a local night school—or even privately as a one-night seminar. You'll increase your exposure, boost your credibility, and make a little extra money in the process.

======= BRIGHT IDEA =======

TELECOMMUNICATIONS CONSULTING

These days, setting up a business phone system is a complex affair. After sorting through a tangle of equipment and a maze of possible configurations, then comparing companies and service packages, one starts to believe the whole business is a full-time job—or even a full-time business.

For a growing number of phone-oriented consultants, it's precisely that. Given all the options businesses have to consider—various companies, sundry equipment, fax and modem hookups, not to mention actual usage—it's no mystery why telecommunications consulting is a growing business.

Telecommunications consultants help clients make sense of their various choices. They can offer objective opinions on equipment and service that regular salespeople cannot. After a system is in place, they teach the staff how to use the phone. Silly as that sounds, today's high-tech phone systems leave many employees in the dark. Features like "barge in" and "orbiting" are not self-explanatory. As one disgruntled office worker put it, "I have a college degree and an executive title, but I can't figure out how to call a client. I doubt that Einstein would be able to use our phone system."

The market for telecommunications services includes hospitals, government offices, small businesses, and even home-based operations.

SPECIALTY ADVERTISING

High Net Profit Before Taxes:	$67,000
Average Net Profit Before Taxes:	$30,000
Minimum Start-up:	$5,000
Average Start-up:	$12,000

If your house is like most people's, it's full of foreign names. Your pens, your calendars, even your potholders sport the names of restaurants, hotels, stores, services, and politicians. Where does all this stuff come from?

From specialty advertising firms, of course. In this country, advertising incentives and premiums account for some $23 billion in sales. Advertising specialties run the gamut from personalized lollipops to custom-engraved clocks. They're given in the hope that one day, perhaps months from now, you'll ask, "What was the name of that business broker in Dubuque?" and you'll find the answer on your felt-tipped pen.

The firms that provide these products often spring from humble beginnings. With just a telephone, business cards, and a case full of samples, you can get a modest start in the specialty advertising game. Overall, success in this business depends as much upon your salesmanship and management ability as it does on the amount of cash you have to spend up front.

The Brokering Trade

A specialty advertising firm acts as a broker between the client company and various manufacturers of specialty items. The firm's main purpose is to devise an effective program that fits the client's budget.

That may sound easy, but it requires some knowledge and skill. There are literally thousands of specialty advertising products on the market. In addition to giveaways like pens, potholders, ice scrapers, and spatulas, there are awards and trophies, client gifts, and premiums (i.e., plastic measuring cups to be given away with boxes of soap). Having a thorough understanding of the options available—as well as the client's goals—is essential.

Those who have the knack, however, enjoy a low-risk venture with outstanding profit potential. Because specialty ad firms only buy products after they've received an order, they seldom get "stuck" with unsalable merchandise.

At the same time, demand for specialty advertising continues to grow. Even in recession years, industry sales remain strong. "Large corporations find that they can spend millions on television ads, and people still don't remember them," explains one successful entrepreneur. "The strength of [the specialty advertising] industry is that corporate America loves specialties. They work."

==================== BRIGHT IDEA ====================

WRITE YOUR OWN RULES

After two consecutive Christmas Eves of frustration, Richard Palackas was fit to be "Scrooged." Thoroughly confused by the directions for putting toys together, Palackas thought, "I can do a better job than that."

So in 1985, the Afton, New York, science teacher started

his part-time product instruction writing service, Saber-
tooth Analysis, from his home. "I started by writing instructions for toy and game manufacturers, and have gone on to
electronics and sporting goods," says Palackas. "What sets
me apart is that I've been trained to deal with children who
can read at an eighth-grade level, which is the level the
average consumer reads at." Forget the reading ability: Most
of us are reduced to an eighth grader's emotional level after
dealing with poorly written instructions.

Though Palackas continues to teach, his writing business often takes up full-time hours. "I put in some seriously
busy days," he says. "There are times when I work until two
or three A.M."

PUBLIC RELATIONS AGENCY

High Net Profit Before Taxes:	$57,000-plus
Average Net Profit Before Taxes:	$36,000
Minimum Start-up:	$10,500
Average Start-up:	$23,000

The business world is wild for free publicity. With the cost of
advertising on the rise, the value of a news story, magazine
article, or television appearance increases daily. Publicity is
not only free, it establishes credibility that advertising can't.
Read an ad that proclaims a restaurant "exquisite," and
you're likely to shrug your shoulders. Read a restaurant review that says the same and you're likely to eat there on your
next lunch hour.

The truth about most free publicity is that it's not free at
all. Corporations, government agencies, politicians, and celebrities all devote substantial sums of money to public relations.

But what exactly is public relations? It's putting a business in the public eye. It's making sure there's media
coverage when the news is good, and keeping the press at
bay when it isn't. To succeed in public relations, you must be
part journalist, part salesperson, and part marketing genius. This is not a job for the slow-witted. Good PR people
always think on their feet.

Skill Is a Must

You don't need much to start a public relations firm. An office (a bedroom or den will do), business stationery, a typewriter, desk, and telephone, are about all you need to set up shop. Beginning equipment and facility requirements are modest in this business.

Skill, on the other hand, is another story. You don't have to have a particular degree or lengthy public relations experience to start your own PR firm. Nonetheless, experience counts. Even limited experience in public relations will help you get the business going. Experience in journalism, marketing, and/or sales is also a plus. Remember that clients are paying you for your expertise. If you know literally nothing about public relations, your services won't be worth much.

Before you strike out on your own, consider taking a course in public relations at a local adult-education program or university extension. Even if you have experience in the field, the more you know, the more valuable your services are.

Choose Your Market

Large public relations firms represent a wide range of clients, but most small firms specialize. Take stock of your local connections. Are you active in the small-business community? Do you work with a lot of charitable organizations? Are you politically active? The safest way to launch a new firm is to use connections you already have.

Once you've decided on a focus, look for new ways to reach your market. Most clients do not choose publicists on the basis of advertising. Referrals and networking are the most common way to develop business, so keep yourself active. Join networking groups, offer to speak at trade association meetings, contact friends and associates for possible client leads.

Above all, be patient. While good publicists make good money once they're established, the going can be tough while building the business. Seasoned PR pros suggest keeping expenses to a minimum and marketing aggressively during the early years. Once the business takes root, however, you can look forward to profits worth publicizing. Average net profits loom near the $40,000 mark, and gross billings of more than $1 million are not uncommon.

GETTING A GRIP

You don't have to be a klutz to slip and fall. In fact, it's happened to most of us. That's why Steven Sharpe, a graduate in hotel/restaurant management, launched Santa Barbara, California-based Slipproof International in 1983. Slipproof is a service designed to remove the slip-and-fall hazards from such environments as commercial kitchens, tile and marble floors, and poolsides.

"The formula, which is applied with applicators and buffers, develops a porous, nonskid surface in the area where it's applied," Sharpe explains. "While the foot would normally hydroplane across the floor, the Slipproof surface causes the foot to grip instead."

A slick floor is more than a nuisance to unsuspecting pedestrians. In commercial settings, it can present an occupational hazard—and a financial liability. You can devise your own formula for taking the slip out of floors or buy into Sharpe's. Through a dealership program, Sharpe teaches would-be slipproofers the technical process and provides marketing information.

POSTING PROFITS

As a rule, the cost of postage goes only one way—up. For businesses that mail thousands of brochures, letters, catalogs, and invoices each year, postage costs can represent a huge annual expenditure. Is there any way for companies to cut the cost of postage?

Yes, and it presents an interesting opportunity for aspiring business owners. Presorting mail may not sound like a lucrative business, but for a handful of businesses that do it well, it can be profitable. Orlando, Florida, entrepreneurs Scott Hart and Quentin Leightey turned their Compusort into a million-dollar business. And no wonder: Their service turns its profits by saving companies money.

Here's how it works: Sorting mail costs the post office time and resources. Therefore, the post office offers a discount on presorted mail—at the time of this writing, four cents on a twenty-five-cent letter. A mid-sized company with a 5,000-piece-per-day mailing, then, could save $200 a day or about $60,000 a year by presorting its outgoing mail.

Most companies forgo the savings to avoid the hassle. But by hiring Compusort, they can have their mail picked up, sorted, and delivered to the post office—and still save money. Compusort splits the four-cent discount with their clients. So that same mid-sized company can save $30,000 a year without lifting a finger. And convenience is only one selling point. Many small companies don't generate the 500-letter-per-day presort minimum by themselves. By pooling their mail through a sorting service, they can take advantage of the presort discount.

Starting a sorting company is relatively easy. In many markets, start-up equipment consists of a vehicle to pick up and drop off mail, a few bins, some sorting machines, and a staff of easily trained employees (who generally work for minimum wage). Otherwise, learning the intricacies of postal regulation and finding the right marketing plan are the two main weapons you'll need. According to Leightey, meticulous attention to customer service is also a must. "In this business, you have to earn the customer's trust every single day," he says. "You've got to go the extra mile."

EXECUTIVE RECRUITING SERVICE

High Net Profit Before Taxes:	$250,000
Average Net Profit Before Taxes:	$80,000
Minimum Start-up:	$16,000
Average Start-up:	$27,000

Two current trends make executive recruiting a promising business opportunity. The first is the growing importance of small business. Years ago, large corporations dominated the employment scene. But today smaller companies are hiring like mad, accounting for most of the job growth that's occurred over the past decade. As a rule, smaller companies need more help in hiring. They have neither the time nor the expertise to make an informed decision, and yet the impact of a poor choice is felt more keenly at a small firm. Meanwhile, corporate downsizing has thousands of qualified executives pounding the pavement. Like any other job seekers, these displaced executives need help finding work—help that regular employment agencies often aren't equipped to provide.

From an entrepreneurial perspective, here's a business that requires a minimal start-up investment and no inventory headaches. Given the right combination of sales and skill, you can bring in six-figure profits after just a few years in business. And there are emotional benefits as well: A good executive recruiter benefits both employer and employee.

Where Agencies Leave Off

An executive recruiting firm is not an employment agency, although the two businesses share some characteristics. Both match job seekers with prospective employers for a fee. At employment agencies the job seeker generally pays the fee, while the employer usually pays the executive search fee. Moreover, a general employment agency deals primarily with jobs that pay $20,000 or less—clerical and administrative work, bookkeeping, and so on. Executive recruiting firms deal with higher-paying managerial and executive positions. Since fees are often based on a percentage of salary, executive recruiters stand to make higher profits per placement.

In exchange for higher fees, however, executive recruiters must know their business. To succeed, you must know the ins and outs of hiring. You must have an understanding of business—on both a general level and in regard to specific clients. Clients expect you to deliver only candidates who are qualified for the position at hand, so it is imperative that you

be able to read a résumé, ask the right questions, check
references, and size up a candidate in an interview.

The markets you'll serve as an executive recruiter are
twofold. On the one hand, you must bring in corporate clients for whom you'll recruit. On the other, you must identify
and attract qualified job candidates. Because both aspects of
the business are critical, the ideal executive recruiter has
marketing skills as well as a knowledge of personnel. If you
aren't a crack marketer (or an experienced personnel coun-
selor), consider hiring people who are. Though executive
recruiting is a growing field, it isn't foolproof. The better your
firm, the better your chances of succeeding.

Small Fish in a Big Pond

According to *Executive Recruiter News*, the newsletter of
executive search, there are some 1,700 search firms doing
business in the United States. Of these, perhaps fewer than
ten are big businesses themselves and routinely handle
multi-million-dollar clients. Most executive recruiters, however, are small businesses that deal with a variety of clients.

Are small firms viable in today's climate? One indication
that they are is the increasing number of independent recruiters who come from big firms. Large executive search
firms have the advantage of being high-profile organizations
with well-known reputations. But, once established, small
firms can offer advantages all their own. As a small company,
you can offer clients more personalized service, especially for
small clients who might get lost in the shuffle at a larger
firm.

To compete effectively, you may also wish to choose a
specialty. Take stock of local businesses. For instance, if
you're located in an area with several small high-tech firms,
consider specializing in executives with computer backgrounds. A specialty can lend your firm credibility, but make
sure the field you choose is wide enough to support your
business and allow for future growth.

ADVERTISING AGENCY

High Net Profit Before Taxes:	$144,000
Average Net Profit Before Taxes:	$100,000
Minimum Start-up:	$23,000
Average Start-up:	$36,000

When most of us think of advertising, we think of huge Madison Avenue corporations cranking out slick, artsy ads for companies like Coca-Cola and General Motors. But of the 5,000-plus advertising agencies in America, only a few have achieved national recognition.

The rest are small agencies—and they're doing quite nicely, thank you. With only a few accounts, many small agencies bill seven figures a year, and some project first-year gross incomes of $150,000 to $300,000. Sales like these may not make you Saachi & Saachi, but they do represent a tidy profit for just about any new business owner.

What Do You Know?

In advertising, skill does count. While the profits can be good on the upside, it's important to consider the downside as well. Without some knowledge of advertising's fundamentals, it is hard to make it in this business.

That isn't to say you can't learn. If you're serious about advertising, but have limited experience in the business, look for ways to improve your knowledge. Classes and seminars are a good start; hands-on experience is even better. Skill and experience are a plus in any business, but in advertising they're a virtual must. Even if you plan to hire those skills you lack (creative skills, for instance), it pays to learn the business from the inside out. The time you spend learning will be paid back in credibility, contacts, and sales.

Inside the Agency

In addition to knowing the business, a new ad agency owner must practice what he or she preaches. Your success depends on your ability to sell your services. Getting your foot in the door is probably the hardest part. Established agency owners recommend lining up at least a few clients before starting the business in earnest. Landing that first client can take some time, so it's best to do your courting while you're still on someone else's payroll.

Across the country, small ad agencies are competing successfully with large firms, but not without savvy. Shrewd management is important—and too often lacking in creative types. Remember that image is all in advertising, so put some thought into your office decor, stationery, and personal attire. Also look for areas of expertise that might give you a competitive edge. In many cities, agencies that specialize in minority advertising are making a splash. So are firms that focus in on a particular segment of the field, such as catalog design.

Overall, the future for independent agencies looks bright. As advertising becomes more and more complicated (and more expensive), companies small and large will continue seeking the expertise of professionals. The challenge for new agencies is keeping up with sophisticated client and consumer markets. Advertising is here to stay, but the face of the business is constantly changing.

=====BRIGHT IDEA=====

ON THE MOVE

When Kim Park married her husband Tony, the couple moved into a new house in Jackson, Tennessee. "I wasn't prepared for the amount of work involved in a move," Kim recalls, "especially when it came to having all the utilities hooked up."

In the midst of this move, the couple saw a news report that mentioned the large number of new companies relocating to the Jackson area. "I immediately thought what a hassle it must be for people to move to an area with which they are totally unfamiliar," says Park. "Even knowing the area and the locations of all the utility companies, I still had spent days trying to get everything taken care of. I figured these people might appreciate a relocation service."

So Park started Trading Places Relocation Services. In planning her new business, Park immediately recognized that she would need the cooperation of the area's utility, cable, water, and telephone services. She met with each of the services and convinced them to cooperate with her. "I explained to them that after a company moved to the area, instead of thirty new customers asking them questions, they would have to deal with only one person—me," says Park. "They saw the benefits immediately."

From the Jackson Chamber of Commerce, Park learned of all the companies planning to move to the area, and began making presentations. Park showed executives in real dollars and man-hours the cost to a business when employees are forced to take care of the details surrounding a move. They were impressed, and Park was in business.

Relocation services like Park's are springing up across the country—and with good reason. The days when wives were available to handle the drudgery of a company move are over. With both men and women working, time spent dealing with a move is time taken away from company business.

In addition to the services that Park provides, some relocation services offer referrals to child care, maid services, and other local vendors. Others provide career and job-placement counseling to the spouses of relocated workers. Whatever the formula, relocation services face a growing market. Americans continue to move, while the time they have to spend on moving dwindles.

NEW CONSTRUCTION INTERIOR CLEANING

High Net Profit Before Taxes:	$42,000
Average Net Profit Before Taxes:	$37,000
Minimum Start-up:	$8,800
Average Start-up:	$14,000

In 1989, an estimated 1.7 million housing units were built in the United States. And when the work was done, they all had one thing in common: They were a mess.

Unbeknownst to many people, there are services that specialize in cleaning new homes after construction is completed. This makes sense if you think about it. After all, someone has to vacuum, mop, shine, polish, and touch-up those houses to a high gloss—and it's a good guess it isn't the average construction worker. In areas where new housing is expanding rapidly, a new construction interior-cleaning business can be both lucrative and simple. All you need is some basic equipment, a willingness to work, and a marketing plan.

Check the Home Front

Before you consider starting a new construction cleaning business, try to determine the sales potential in your community. Not every area has enough new housing to support this type of service, and you can't count on being the only game in town. Here's a quick way to estimate the market in your area:

Scan the Yellow Pages for home builder listings. Eliminate those builders who are based outside your immediate area (typically, about 30 percent). Of the remaining builders, figure that 40 percent will be low-volume operators who should also be eliminated. This will leave you with 60 percent of the remaining builders to work with. If that 60 percent equals only five or ten companies, new construction cleaning may not be the business for you.

Another quick check: Cruise your surrounding neighborhood. Are there new housing tracts being built? Is there room for more tracts like them? In established neighborhoods, how many new houses per block are being built? Contact your city manager or county clerk's office and ask how many new building permits are being issued. If pickings are slim, look for another business, or consider doing this one as an adjunct to another business—window cleaning or janitorial work, for example.

In a Day's Work

What do new construction cleaning services do? After the subcontractors have completed their jobs and before the house is turned over to the buyer, the cleaning service does some finetuning. They clean up paint that was put in the wrong places, along with stucco, cement, glue, dirt, mud, tire and heel marks, etc. In short, they put the house in order.

To accomplish this task, several pieces of equipment are needed. A company vehicle is essential, though it doesn't have to be fancy. Since most new homes do not have electricity, a 3,500- to 4,000-watt generator is in order to run your equipment. A floor scrubber with a sanding disk will remove oil and paint stains from concrete areas; new carpets get the once-over with an upright vacuum. For dirt and spills an upright can't reach, you will also need a wet-dry vacuum. Additionally, plan to buy ladders, mops, buckets, brooms, window scrapers, squeegees, and miscellaneous hand tools for odd jobs.

The work itself is fairly straightforward—and fairly hard. Once you establish yourself with steady clients, however, the profits are ample. Better still, you can expand a new construction cleaning service to include other types of work: cleaning homes for resale, office cleaning, and "boxing out," or removing boxes and trash from the interior of a new site.

===================== BRIGHT IDEA =====================

TRANSLATION SERVICE

Americans are notoriously single-lingual. For most of us, the attitude is "English only," and for years we've gotten away with it. But as more and more businesses consider expanding into international markets, the need for translation is all too obvious. And the demand for translation services has never been greater.

This at a time when the American translation business is largely a cottage industry. Freelancers dominate, while the top ten translation companies worldwide control less than 1 percent of the $10 billion global market. Translated into entrepreneurial terms, this means unique opportunities for business-minded translators.

Freelancing continues to be a viable option, particularly

for those with limited cash reserves (and true fluency in a foreign language). With a word processor, a telephone, and some contacts, you can start taking in work immediately.

But perhaps the most interesting opportunities lie in larger ventures—not necessarily multinational conglomerates, but organized companies with sound marketing and management, and the ability to work in several languages. To size up the market in your community, contact your local chamber of commerce—or the U.S. Department of Commerce—and ask for lists of businesses in your area that are involved in international dealings. No matter where you are, chances are good that demand for translation is on the rise.

TRANSPORTATION FREIGHT BROKERAGE

High Net Profit Before Taxes:	$100,000
Average Net Profit Before Taxes:	$85,000
Minimum Start-up:	$6,500
Average Start-up:	$10,000

Everything that's bought or sold in America was once a piece of freight. By plane, boat, truck, or train, every salable item somehow gets from manufacturer to wholesaler to retailer and finally to the consumer. Furthermore, plenty of shippable goods go into a finished piece. For example, a sofa consists of wood from one source, fabric from another, and stuffing from still another. All converge at the sofa manufacturing plant—all thanks to the shipping business.

With so many goods going from one place to another, it's no wonder that shipping represents an enormous industry in the United States. And the business consists of more than carriers and shippers: There is also a hidden market for freight brokers, companies that match shippers with the appropriate carriers.

Why the need for a middleman? Shipping can be a complex affair for the uninitiated. Finding the right means of transportation, contacting individual carriers, and comparing estimates takes time. When a crisis arises—due to bad weather, for instance, or a strike—a freight broker can find alternative means of shipping. He or she can also coordinate shipments to save clients money. Because it's their business, freight brokers can handle all of these tasks efficiently.

And in the process, brokers can make good money. Though profits vary widely, it's not uncommon for an established broker to earn $100,000 a year. The starting investment is enticingly small: You can get started for less than $10,000.

Setting Up Shop

The shipping business has a language all its own. Like any other idiom, it takes a while to learn. But don't confuse new terminology with complication. The shipping business is, at root, as simple as getting goods from one point to another. If you can accomplish this, you can master the business. The details will fall into place as you become more familiar with the business.

As in any business, experience helps. If you're totally lost on the subject of shipping, consider taking a job at a freight brokerage or shipping company. Or read up on the subject at your local library. Established freight brokers report that this business isn't difficult to learn, and a little knowledge goes a long way.

You don't need much in the way of equipment or facilities to start a freight brokerage. If zoning laws permit, you can operate out of your home—or rent a modest office on the cheap. You will need a phone, two Rolodexes (one for carriers, one for clients), a desk, business stationery, a few reference books, and very little else.

There is no magic formula for making sales in the freight business. Many start-up brokers simply trace manufacturers' phone numbers from product labels and call to offer their services. Other sources of potential clients include the Yellow Pages and the local chamber of commerce. Direct contact with potential clients seems to be the most effective means of promoting a new freight brokerage, so polish up your phone manner and start dialing.

MISCELLANEOUS SERVICES

VIDEO PRODUCTION COMPANY

High Net Profit Before Taxes:	$50,000
Average Net Profit Before Taxes:	$30,000
Minimum Start-up:	$16,000
Average Start-up:	$25,000

If you've always dreamed of becoming a professional film-maker and bringing in star-quality profits, this could be the business for you. New state-of-the-art equipment makes the video business accessible to almost anyone. And it's possible to launch your own video production service part-time from your home.

We found one entrepreneur who turned a $1,500 part-time business investment into $85,000 in less than ten months. He concentrated on five major market areas:

1) Recording inventory for insurance purposes.
2) Taping weddings, birthdays, and other celebrations.
3) Video documentation of legal proceedings.
4) Video tours of property for local real estate agencies.
5) Covering exhibits, sales, and teaching presentations, conventions, and other speaking engagements.

The intricacies of videography do involve skill, talent, and training. However, thanks to technological advances, video mastery is easier—and cheaper—to attain than ever. With a little training and practice, you too can produce professional results.

Everyone's in the Movies

The two major markets for a videotaping service are individual consumer and commercial. Individual consumers may hire videographers to document weddings, bar mitzvahs, birthdays, anniversaries, graduations, family reunions, and other important events. Recently, videographers have begun producing life reviews, documentaries of their clients' lives. These video histories make great entertainment for birthday or retirement parties, and represent a bit of family history that can be passed down through the generations.

Videographers usually go "on location" to clients' homes or party sites. However, you may also set up a studio or convert a room in your house for live studio portraits. "In-house" tapings are also ideal for video wills, video letters, or any type of information someone wishes taped. People in the entertainment industry may also prove to be a fertile market: They often use videos as a kind of résumé.

Commercially speaking, there's a raft of opportunities open to able videographers. Ad agencies regularly use video to produce commercials. Businesses and schools often use videos for training purposes. Promotional films are an important PR device for corporations, newspapers and magazines, and real estate offices.

Videotaping has become an important issue in the insurance business. The videotaped testimony of a deceased patient recently helped secure one of the largest out-of-court settlements ever awarded. In a similar vein, many doctors are now videotaping surgery to protect themselves against malpractice suits—and insurance companies are offering them discounts to do so.

Start with the Basics

You won't find any shortage of video equipment on the market today. But with all the "goodies" available, be careful not to get carried away. Buy only the bare essentials to start, renting those pieces you need occasionally. Invest in a quality camera, but don't spend all your start-up funds. Remember that a good portion of your initial investment should go toward advertising and promotions. As you bring in more money, you can reinvest in additional equipment.

Among the extras you'll want to consider: remote lights, remote microphones, tripods, VCR decks (at least two), audiocassette recorder, videotape eraser (degausser), sound mixer, and picture enhancer. Until you buy these extras, many may be available through rental companies.

================ BRIGHT IDEA ================

BALLOON WRAP

Throw away the tape, the ribbon, and the wrapping paper. One of the hottest new businesses for the 1990s is balloon wrapping—and it eliminates the need for old-fashioned gift-wrapping methods.

According to Les Wigger, president of Yorba Linda, California-based Balloon Wrap Inc., the balloon-wrapping principle is really quite simple. "We wrap gifts like stuffed animals, clothes, or flowers in a balloon instead of an ordinary box. The objects we can wrap are limited only by the imagination," he says. "Our patent-pending machine is designed to leave a four-and-a-quarter-inch space for the insertion of the items, and then the opening is cinched with a special tie."

The balloon-wrapping machines are sold for an average price of $1,500, and they can be set up in many different business environments. Wrapping machines are often the focus of kiosks and carts found in malls during the holiday seasons, but they can also be used in department stores, flower shops, or home-based businesses. Wigger contends that the most lucrative area for balloon wrappers is special event wrapping. "Centerpieces average about $35, but wrappers can charge as much as $150 for the most ornate designs."

The price for a standard balloon wrap ranges from $3 to

$10, depending on the location of the business and the nature of the gift. Wigger says, "Balloon wrappers can start out with the balloon machine and slowly build their businesses by selling the products they wrap."

ONE-HOUR PHOTO PROCESSING SERVICE

High Net Profit Before Taxes:	$100,000
Average Net Profit Before Taxes:	$65,000
Minimum Start-up:	$185,000
Average Start-up:	$240,000

Here's a business that allows you to develop high-quality snapshots in well under an hour, and high-margin revenues in well under a year. You do not need professional expertise in photography to open your own photo-finishing minilab. In fact, few minilab owners have photography backgrounds. What you do need is business savvy and the ability to keep a production line running smoothly.

New high-tech equipment makes fast turnaround times—and high profits—possible. In the right location, with less than a thousand square feet and a good marketing plan, an independent with little or no photo-finishing expertise could expect an annual gross in the $200,000 range. Some minilab owners we talked to are projecting nets of $150,000 after just two months in business.

The One-Hour Revolution

In 1978, Noritsu American Corporation (then known as NAC) came out with the Quick Service System (QSS)—a process that changed the face of the photo-finishing business. Before the QSS, quick photo-finishing took a minimum of two days. Now, the QSS can transform a roll of 110, 126, or 135 color film into completely dry snapshots in a total of twenty-eight minutes. Standard color negatives can be run back through the minilab for reprints in a total of ten minutes. And the entire procedure is automated.

Following the success of the Noritsu system, other manufacturers have jumped into the fray. This spells good news for the retailer entering the market today, since these manufacturers will be in hot competition for shares of the hardware market.

In fact, the current technology and manufacturer support is so good these days that you could start a minilab business with virtually no technical background. "I thought cyan was a country," one operator joked, "but I'm still making money."

Naturally, good equipment doesn't come cheap. Your initial cash outlay will probably exceed $200,000, especially since a prime location is important in this business. But the operators we spoke with reported an unusually rapid return on investment. Many minilabs have been operating in the black from their third month in business—some even from their first.

Where the Growth Is

According to the operators we contacted, instant processing is comparable to standard professional processing in terms of quality. If standard processing were a 10 quality-wise, instant processing might be an 8.5. For professional photographers, this level of quality might not be high enough. But for the vast majority of amateurs, the quality is more than adequate—and amateurs of this sort make up a huge percentage of the overall photo-processing market.

Since convenience is your primary selling point, consider your location carefully. If they're affordable, malls can be ideal locations for minilabs, since they provide a wealth of foot traffic as well as a place for clients to browse while their prints are being processed. Stand-alone and strip-center locations are also workable as long as they offer plenty of convenient parking.

Also concentrate on maintaining smooth operations. Volume is one key to this business, so make sure your production is running at full capacity. Remember, too, that speed is a must. If you can't deliver the prints within the promised hour, you run the risk of alienating customers. Once your operations are established, you can operate your minilab as an absentee owner.

=================== BRIGHT IDEA ===================

FINANCIAL PLANNING

The world of personal finance has become so complicated that the average person needs help. Financial planners assist clients in everything from calculating net worth to budgeting income and choosing the right investments.

Financial planning is a growing field. There are roughly 150,000 financial planners in the United States, compared to just a handful twenty years ago. One reason for this growth is high earning potential. Good financial planners charge hourly fees of $80 to $175, or make a mint in commissions. And, outside of any educational expenses, start-up investments are low. You can start a financial planning consultancy for less than $10,000 and still bring in an attractive profit.

To succeed, you will need some expertise. Most financial planners come from backgrounds in insurance, accounting, financial services, or law. While these backgrounds are helpful, almost anyone can become a qualified financial planner through course study. Many state and private colleges offer courses; home-study opportunities may be available as well.

PRIVATE MAILBOX SERVICE

High Net Profit Before Taxes:	$57,000
Average Net Profit Before Taxes:	$39,000
Minimum Start-up:	$17,000
Average Start-up:	$30,000

If you think simplicity is a virtue, this is the business for you. There is no inventory, little maintenance, and no need for full-time employees. Moreover, what work there is is easy: You simply receive incoming mail, sort it, and place it in the proper mailbox.

For this, you can net annual profits of $40,000 or more. Add a few auxiliary services like photocopies, fax transmissions, packing and shipping, word processing, and so on, and you can increase your profits even further. Successful mailbox operations around the country are giving the old P.O. a run for its money—and in a few areas, the market is still wide open.

Who Rents Mailboxes?

Most people don't associate profits with mailboxes, but nonetheless, the private mailbox business is thriving. Just who rents mailboxes? Individuals who spend a lot of time away from home—students, salespeople, and so on—often rent boxes to save themselves the hassle of starting and stopping their mail service. Renting a mailbox also ensures that someone is there to receive packages or important correspondence.

Small business owners represent the largest segment of the market. In some cases, mailbox service speeds delivery. In other cases, a business might prefer to keep its office address anonymous. Home-based businesses often use private mailboxes to simulate office addresses. Instead of listing his or her home address, a business owner can simply list the street address of the mailbox service along with a "suite" number that corresponds with his box. A permanent mailbox address also provides continuity to businesses that move locations frequently.

What About the Post Office?

Isn't the post office fairly stiff competition for this kind of service? Yes—and no. In areas where post office boxes are easily obtained, this might be true. But in many areas, there are long waiting lists for post office boxes. If you aren't sure which category your community falls into, visit your local post office and apply for a box. Their response should tell you whether or not your area will have pent-up demand for private postal boxes.

In choosing a location for your business, consider location carefully. Convenience is a priority for your customers, so look for a spot with plenty of parking and easy access from the street. Remember that businesses are a good source of clients. Check out the number of home-based businesses as well as offices and shops.

Also consider the desirability of your address, since your address is a major marketing point. Ideal metropolitan and suburban business locations are those with prime addresses situated near small/medium-sized operations off the main drag. High-rise condos and apartments nearby (along with upper-middle-class residential neighborhoods) are also a plus, as you're maximizing the market potential for individuals and home-based businesses.

===================== BRIGHT IDEA =====================

PERENNIAL THANK-YOUS

Maybe it doesn't grow on trees, but brothers Kevin and Patrick Ahern have found a way to make money grow from plants. The Aherns are the brains behind Thank You Plants, an Encinitas, California-based gift and customer tracking company.

Kevin came up with the idea while working for another company. That firm sent its customers plants as gestures of thanks. Kevin and his brother Patrick were so impressed with the idea that they decided to launch a company based solely on that service.

Most of the Aherns' fifty clients are auto dealerships. Recent customers are sent a gift plant and a follow-up survey on the dealership's service. The Aherns plan to expand their clientele to include individuals, retailers, and general businesses.

LAWN MAINTENANCE SERVICE

High Net Profit Before Taxes:	$67,000-plus
Average Net Profit Before Taxes:	$35,000
Minimum Start-up:	$12,000
Average Start-up:	$23,000

Lawn-care entrepreneurs are seeing green—in more ways than one. As leisure time shrinks, more and more people are turning to professional lawn-care services to mow, fertilize, water, and chemically treat their lawns. And the residential market is only part of the picture. Commercial property—from office parks to condo complexes—also requires outside lawn maintenance. All told, lawn care and management represent a $2,8 billion business in the U.S. And the field continues to grow at a rate of 15 to 20 percent per year.

Lawn Maintenance vs. Chemical Care

There are two basic business concepts in the lawn-care field: maintenance and chemical care. Lawn-maintenance services mow and fertilize lawns, and often provide basic landscape maintenance like hedge clipping, collecting leaves, and so on. Chemical lawn-care companies simply apply fertilizers and pesticides to clients' lawns five or six times a year.

You can launch either type of operation on a part-time basis. Since all of your work will be done on location, lawn-care services are easily adapted to the home office. Equipment needs for either business are similar: pick-up truck, telephone with an answering machine or answering service, chemical spreader, aerator, and a supply of chemicals. If you're starting a maintenance-oriented service, you will also need a tractor-style lawn mower, self-propelled power mower, gas or electric grass trimmer, and various hand tools.

Testing the Waters

Equipment won't make the business work, however. Marketing is the most essential ingredient in any lawn-care business. Before you get started, select your target market carefully. Will you cater to more residential clients, or stress the commercial? Is the neighborhood you live in a good target, or are you better off seeking another community?

The most promising neighborhoods are densely populated and middle- or upper-middle-class. Working couples are ideal clients, as are elderly people. Commercially speaking, almost any patch of lawn is fair game. Corporations, schools, shopping centers, malls, hospitals, and city governments are always looking for more cost-effective grounds maintenance.

New housing tracts or office parks are obvious targets for your services, but don't overlook established communities— even those that are already serviced by other companies. Customer loyalty runs high in this business, but folks may be willing to switch if they aren't getting adequate service. The biggest complaint among lawn-care customers? Lack of weed control.

=======BRIGHT IDEA=======

HIT THE CEILING

A cleaner's work is never done. The latest evidence: a new service that specializes in cleaning ceilings. That's right. It's not enough to clean your desk, your walls, your carpet. Now, your ceiling must also be spotlessly white.

And with good reason. According to Kaaydah Schatten of Ceiling Doctor International, Inc. in Toronto, "Most ceilings are filthy." Schatten explains that dirt and bacteria rise with hot air and stick to the ceiling. Over the course of years, buildup can be downright disgusting.

Schatten discovered the problem while renovating old houses. Ceilings, she noted, often had to be torn out. "At that time, I thought, 'If someone could figure out how to clean a ceiling, they'd make a million dollars,'" Schatten recalls. So she set out to develop her own process.

Today, Schatten's high-pressure dry-chemical cleaning equipment is the basis for her Ceiling Doctor service, as well as franchises across Canada, the U.S., and Japan. While most ceiling work is currently industrial and commercial, Schatten anticipates a future in the residential market as well. Like clean carpets and clean walls, once clean ceilings become the standard, there will be no turning back.

MOBILE LOCKSMITHING

High Net Profit Before Taxes:	$69,000-plus
Average Net Profit Before Taxes:	$50,000
Minimum Start-up:	$12,000
Average Start-up:	$26,000

Just about anything you value has a lock on it: your home, your car, your bicycle, your file cabinet. We're a security-conscious society—and rightfully so. Crime is everywhere these days. Discouraging thieves with locks, bolts, and other security devices is not only sensible, it's common sense.

Which is why locksmithing is a solid business opportunity. Today's locksmith is likely to be part mathematician, part electronics whiz. Items currently on the market include locks that only open using coded magnetic cards or respond only to a specific human voice. Time was, the local locksmith could get by by being a tinkerer who could even repair your toaster if need be. But the days are numbered for these old-timers, who are giving way to a new breed of security professionals.

Keys to Success

Locksmith operations don't have to be large to make money. Many are one-person operations, perhaps with family members helping out. Using a van as a mobile workshop and a home office as a base of operations, a well-organized established locksmith can gross $50,000 to $70,000 per year and net about $25,000.

However, some locksmiths are thinking big, with multiple van units and retail locations as home bases. Considering that most of the competition comes from mom-and-pop operations, ambitious, business-minded individuals have a real opportunity to prosper in this business. What it takes is aggressive marketing and promotion, strong management skills, and a determination to make the venture grow.

A Lock on the Market

Virtually everyone is a potential customer for a locksmithing service. Anyone who owns a home, lives in an apartment, runs a business, or drives a car is a prime prospect. So are schools, churches, government institutions, and a wide variety of other commercial and industrial accounts.

Seek out opportunities for sales. For instance, new homeowners need locks changed once contractors are through. Who wants unauthorized keys floating around town in the hands of workers who may be unscrupulous? People who live in older homes or apartments may want to upgrade their security by adding dead bolt locks or installing a floor safe.

Concentrate on lucrative commercial accounts. As one owner put it, "It takes me five minutes to make a key for someone who walks in off the street, and I make $1.25 in the same time it would take to sell $500 worth of hardware to a commercial account." Sources to consider: banks, small businesses, office complexes, and warehouses.

Opening the Door

Before you launch a locksmithing service, check out your local market. How many locksmiths are operating in your area? An industry rule of thumb is that there is one locksmith for every 30,000 people in most major markets. Thus there is plenty of room for more—especially in major cities with heavy concentrations of industrial and commercial accounts.

Find out who your potential clients might be. Your local chamber of commerce should be able to provide you with lists of businesses in your area. Your board of realtors should have lists of apartment owners and can point you toward the local welcome wagon, newcomers' clubs, and other sources of residential business.

In addition to market information, you'll need technical knowledge to launch your service. You can learn the trade and pay the rent by working as a locksmith apprentice for a year or two. Ask your local community college or night school if they offer courses in locksmithing. Courses are also available through correspondence from the Belsaw Institute, and the Locksmithing Institute, to name just a few sources of training. The Associated Locksmiths of America also offer seminars and workshops on the locksmithing business. Learning the locksmithing business will take time, but as you learn the technical aspects, you'll have time to gather information on your market and construct a viable plan.

The Image Angle

When you're ready to start, pay close attention to your professional image. Many established locksmiths overlook this factor altogether, and this limits their profit potential.

As a mobile locksmith, you will gain entry to people's homes and workplaces. The more professional and trustworthy you are, the more likely they'll be to contact you in the future. Quick, efficient service; a clean, well-maintained van; and a company uniform all lend an air of professionalism to your operations—at relatively little cost to you.

In the beginning, you can keep start-up costs down by working out of a van, using your home as an office. But to improve your visibility—and increase your volume—opening a shop is a wise down-the-road move. A fixed retail location with visible signs will improve your reputation and your professional image. If you're interested in maximum profits, a retail base is the way to go.

Though starting small in this business is possible, don't start out with too little capital. Locksmithing is not a get-rich-quick business in which anyone with a little money and a few tools can hit the jackpot. Equipment, training, multiple units, and retail locations cost money, but for most savvy operators, they're well worth the investment. There is excellent money to be made in locksmithing—for those who are professional, capable, and well trained.

========BRIGHT IDEA========

CALENDAR PUBLISHING

What has twelve full-color pictures and keeps you organized? A calendar, of course. Americans are so preoccupied with time that they place great emphasis on its presentation. Watches are a veritable fashion statement nowadays! Little wonder, then, that we give almost as much consideration to the calendars on our walls as we do to our living-room furniture. The array of today's calendars—from Picasso to penguins—bedazzles the eye and entices the wallet. In fact, the calendar has become so popular in the last ten years, it is literally an art form. Calendars are also the basis for some very successful businesses.

Calendar publishing, once the domain of printers who sold inexpensively made calendars as an advertising vehicle for their clients, is now a booming business in its own right. Estimated sales for 1990 calendars exceed $1.3 billion, according to Hallmark Cards. That's almost three times the amount sold five years ago, when calendars brought in $500 million. If you count "free" calendars used as advertising premiums, calendar sales add up to nearly $2 billion.

Patricia Pompili and Spencer Sokale, co-owners of Landmark Calendars in Novato, California, started out with $10,000 and a good idea. Today, their company has 100 employees and 350 different calendar titles. Neither Pompili nor Sokale had previous calendar publishing experience when they started the business in 1979. Pompili was a schoolteacher and Sokale had started several different businesses.

Their first venture was a calendar of twelve historic pictures of the Golden Gate Bridge. "Spencer had bought part of the Golden Gate Bridge cable which is replaced every twenty to thirty years, and he was also given some photographs of its construction," explains Pompili. "We used to look at them all the time, and were fascinated by the process." Those pictures became the first calendar. During their first year in business, they sold 15,000 calendars to elementary schools for use as fund-raisers. By contrast, they expect to sell $18 million to $20 million worth of calendars in 1990.

Calendars are moneymakers, though the outcome of a calendar venture depends largely on you. It takes considerable effort at the beginning to get a calendar off the ground. The more steps you can handle yourself, the lower your costs will be. In addition to labor costs, you will have to consider up-front costs like printing and graphics. Since calendars are typically produced at least a year in advance, you will be spending money that may not be recouped for twelve to eighteen months.

As a beginner, you will want to call on individual stores in your neighborhood to show off your calendar. If it's a calendar with scenes from your own town or county, so much the better. Another important way to get your calendar noticed is the trade show circuit. There are numerous national and regional gift and stationery shows where hopeful unknowns display their calendars and see what the competition is doing.

KITCHEN REMODELING SERVICE

High Net Profit Before Taxes:	$93,000
Average Net Profit Before Taxes:	$74,000
Minimum Start-up:	$85,000
Average Start-up:	$145,000

Given the high price of new construction, many home-buyers are opting for older homes. Generally speaking, older homes are a bargain. Living rooms age well. Bedrooms hold up over the years. Dining rooms don't deteriorate. Older kitchens, on the other hand, usually need help.

Today, remodeling is a $12.6 billion market, with kitchen remodeling representing 16 percent of the overall picture. In the past few years, this industry has experienced an annual growth rate of almost 20 percent. And this trend promises to continue as working couples find less and less time to do their own remodeling.

Just the Kitchen, Thanks

Although the future looks bright for the remodeling industry in general, many smart entrepreneurs are specializing in kitchens. Why? For one thing, consumers are demanding more from their kitchens. They want attractive cabinets, clean countertops, and state-of-the-art appliances. They want kitchens that are livable, and that means well-planned space, new fixtures, and modern decor. A worn-out kitchen can date a home like virtually no other room can (bathrooms excluded); a newly remodeled kitchen can add substantially to the resale value of a home.

Kitchen remodelers offer a variety of services. A quick overhaul might include replacing the countertops and refacing the cabinets, in which the cabinet doors are replaced but the cabinets themselves left intact. Refacing costs about one-third what replacement would. More extensive jobs might involve constructing an "island" in the center of the kitchen for preparing food, or rewiring a kitchen for electric appliances. By specializing in kitchens only, remodeling services can offer more products and greater expertise—just what this market is looking for.

Do the Job Right

This isn't a business for the unskilled. The best preparation is to work for a construction or remodeling company first to get a feel for the tasks at hand. If you're hopeless with a hammer or saw, you can still break into the business as a broker/contractor. You would market remodeling services, then hire employees to perform the work, or contract out to other businesses. Even if you do perform the work yourself, you may contract specialty jobs out—electrical work, for instance.

Remodelers who do most of their own work should expect to spend about $75,000 on starting equipment, inventory, facility, and leasehold improvements. This would include a good used pick-up or van for transportation of tools and raw materials.

Though this may sound like a lot of money to invest, being able to do the job right will give you an advantage over the established competition. Many consumers are wary of remodeling contractors. They worry that the contractor they hire will be unreliable or unskilled. Having a well-maintained vehicle, proper tools, and a well-chosen selection of goods will help establish you as a capable professional.

Expand into Bathrooms

As your business expands, consider adding bathrooms to your repertoire. Like kitchens, bathrooms in older homes usually need a little sprucing up. And you'll use many of the same tools and equipment you would in redoing a kitchen. According to one national survey, kitchen remodeling jobs will exceed the number of housing starts by more than twice; bath remodeling jobs will exceed housing starts by almost 50 percent.

REFERRAL SERVICE

High Net Profit Before Taxes:	$90,000
Average Net Profit Before Taxes:	$50,000
Minimum Start-up:	$5,895
Average Start-up:	$10,730

On one hand, there's a service boom. Thousands of new services are cropping up in fields as specialized and obscure as pet-sitting, plant-watering, and personal shopping. But on the other hand, consumers can't always locate the service they need. Why? Some can't find the right listing in the Yellow Pages. Others want a way to screen services without tracking down and interviewing dozens of candidates.

This problem has opened the door for a new breed of service business: the referral service. For instance, pet owners in search of reliable sitters can call the National Association of Pet Sitters for a referral in their area. Southern California brides-to-be can call The Wedding Guild for help in locating a variety of wedding-related services. Now, when you want to find a good restaurant, locate the movie you want to see, ferret out the right roommate, or track down a medical expert, you can enlist the help of a referral service.

Referral services aren't limited to consumers; business owners also represent a ripe market for these services. Every time a service refers a consumer to a company, it provides a form of advertising. By associating themselves with a referral service, companies are almost guaranteed increased business and sales volume.

Room to Expand

The referral business is just starting to take off in this country, so there's plenty of room for innovation in the field. And since a referral business can be started easily from home with a minimal amount of equipment and money, it is fast becoming a popular field. Start-up costs for a home-based referral business are usually less than $5,000.

"If you have an extra bedroom, a corner of a playroom, or even a large closet where you can install a phone, answering machine, computer, and worktable, then this business can easily be run from your home," says Patti Moran, founder and executive director of the National Association of Pet Sitters (NAPS). "In fact, I'd recommend it. As the business grows and more space and additional help is needed, then the business can be moved to an [outside] office."

Even if you do start out in an office, overhead costs are generally low. Again, equipment needs are minimal, and you don't have to start out with extras like toll-free service.

Valuable Information

The core of a good referral service is its list of vendors. According to David Hollies, owner of Home Connections in Silver Spring, Maryland, careful screening is a must. Home Connections provides homeowners with information on home improvement contractors and repairpeople. Before a vendor can be listed with the service, Hollies and his staff make sure it has the required licenses and insurance. "We also contact the local Better Business Bureau and consumer agencies to see what the company's complaint records are," he says.

The best way to check a company's history, according to Hollies, is to contact people who have used that company's services and ask them how the company handled the work. "The most important thing is past customer references," he explains. Some of the things Hollies and his staff look for are whether the workers arrived on time, whether they completed the job on schedule and at the estimated price, and whether the contractor was willing to answer questions.

Thus, when consumers call Home Connections, they get more than a fast referral. Home Connections provides valuable information—information that can save the customer hours of research and the potential headache of hiring an unreliable service.

Where the Profits Are

Currently, Home Connections has more than 1,000 referral categories and gives an average of 10,000 referrals a year. The service is free to consumers. Hollies charges vendors a per-lead fee of $3 to $120, depending on the type of work. Gross sales for the first year were only a few thousand dollars, but Hollies expects second-year gross sales to be around $130,000.

Per-lead fees are one option. Another is charging an annual fee, as does The Wedding Guild in Orange, California. The Wedding Guild is operated from a retail facility. Qualifying vendors provide lists of services, samples and/or pictures, price lists, addresses, and phone numbers. This information is stored at The Wedding Guild's library, where brides- and grooms-to-be peruse it at their leisure. Annual membership at The Wedding Guild costs vendors $600 to $1,200.

In its first four years of operation, The Wedding Guild has referred more than $75 million worth of business to its members. The Guild serves an average of 50 to 100 brides each week, and many vendors receive as much as 75 percent of their business from the Guild.

Annual fees are the most common sales method for referral services. Under this system, the owner does not have to keep precise records of how many times a company's services were referred to customers, or how many times consumers actually used the services. Annual fees are also advantageous to vendors: They don't have to contend with complicated bookkeeping systems, either.

It is also possible to operate on a commission basis. At Spa-Finders Travel Arrangement Ltd., operators book reservations at spas around the world. For every reservation the company books, it receives a 20 percent commission from the spa. According to owner Jeffrey Joseph, Spa-Finders provides customers with the information they need to choose the right spa vacation—or no spa vacation at all. Clients call in on a toll-free line and are under no obligation to book. Many do, however. In 1989, Spa-Finders booked more than 5,000 reservations and generated sales of approximately $7 million.

Riding the Service Wave

The more aware the public becomes of referral services, the larger the industry will grow. After all, referral services provide a needed bridge between individual vendors and customers who want their services. Without them, consumers waste time locating the right services, and small service businesses agonize over finding affordable advertising. Referral services create a win-win-win situation, and who knows? Perhaps the referral business will be the biggest winner of all.

===================== BRIGHT IDEA =====================

FOR ART'S SAKE

If you're interested in purchasing a work of art, Corinne Shane is interested in you. Shane, president of InvestinArt in New York City, will search galleries, auctions, and art dealers to find the perfect piece of art to fit a client's image and wallet—whether the client is an individual or a large corporation.

Shane started her venture into the art business from her home eight years ago to take advantage of what she terms an explosion of interest in art, on the part of businesses as well as individuals. From the beginning, she's used her own money to finance her business.

The name "InvestinArt" accurately describes just what Shane does. "I help anybody who is interested in buying art find the right investment for the image they want to present," she says. "We sit down and talk it over to see what it is they like, or what they don't like, and we start from there."

Perhaps the major attraction of Shane's service is the price. "The price varies, but in general, it is a very small markup," says Shane. "We don't have the overhead galleries have; they sometimes have to mark a piece of art up 100 to 200 percent."

Shane's prices, as well as her attention to each client, have created a successful business that thrives on word-of-mouth advertising. In fact, Shane is thinking of installing an unlisted number because "I only have time to deal with people who are serious about buying art."

BURGLAR ALARM SALES AND INSTALLATION

High Net Profit Before Taxes:	$100,000
Average Net Profit Before Taxes:	$40,000
Minimum Start-up:	$5,000
Average Start-up:	$30,000

According to government statistics, 3 million burglaries are committed each year. Who's responsible? By and large, burglars are not slick professionals with high-tech equipment and a million tricks. They're kids under 25 who resort to simple breaking and entering.

Although there is no easy "cure" for crime, more and more people are using burglar alarms as deterrents against theft. This is true in both the industrial and residential markets. With so many women in the work force, few houses are occupied during the day. In an empty house, break-ins and other emergencies can go undetected, leaving homeowners feeling insecure and unsettled—ideal candidates for a security system.

What Is Security?

The alarm industry is a diverse one. It includes such services as burglary and robbery control, monthly central switchboard monitoring services, entry monitoring, medical and other emergency alert services, energy use monitoring, and fire-related security services, such as smoke detection, sprinkler, and extinguisher maintenance.

Some companies specialize in one or two service areas, while others cover the whole range. In most cases, the bulk of the business lies in sales and installation of electronic security alarm devices for protection against theft.

The industrial, commercial, and residential markets are all potentially profitable, but the greatest growth area is in residential sales. Initially alarm companies targeted only affluent homeowners, but that slant is shifting. As prices on alarm systems drop (some are available for as little as $500 to $800), more middle-income homeowners and apartment dwellers are signing up for service.

You can learn the skills you'll need to start your own alarm business easily by working in the field for a time. Once you've gathered some basic technical and sales knowledge, start-up is relatively simple. You can work out of your home to start if you have reliable transportation and an answering service.

PEST CONTROL

High Net Profit Before Taxes:	$270,360
Average Net Profit Before Taxes:	$97,150
Minimum Start-up:	$16,000
Average Start-up:	$30,400

When people look forward to the pitter-patter of little feet around their homes, they do not envision those feet attached to six- or eight-legged creatures. No one likes pests. At their best, they are unsightly, unnerving, and generally creepy. At worst, they pose a health hazard and/or a threat of permanent damage to home and garden.

Stamping out irritating pests may not be glamorous work, but it is a necessary and valuable service for which homeowners and businesses alike are willing to pay handsomely. Currently, there are over 9,000 pest-control operators in the United States with annual billings of over $2 billion.

Most Start Out Small

Most of the nation's pest-control operators have fewer than five employees. In fact, many got their start with little more than a gallon of pesticide, a few sprayers, and an operator's license.

Starting out this way is virtually impossible in today's market. Not only will you face tough penalties if you're in violation of government regulations, but you also run the risk of a lawsuit if toxic chemicals are improperly applied. Your own health may be in danger. Coping with the high cost of insurance, tight government regulations, and a buying public wary of toxic chemicals is part and parcel of the business these days. Keeping yourself on solid legal and ethical footing is a must. And so is maintaining a professional image. Invest in the proper equipment and training, a presentable vehicle, and a capable staff. Your customers will feel better—and so will you.

To start a legitimate pest-control business, you must become a licensed pest-control technician. That means going to work for someone else for a few years in order to get the proper experience. This may seem like a lot of time to invest, but the education is essential. Remember, the more you know, the safer and more credible your business will be.

Still Room for Newcomers

The days when consumers would hire just anyone to come in and spray for pests may be over, but the pest-control business is still within reach of the small operator.

The trick is not to underestimate your start-up costs. With insurance, licenses, rent, equipment, and supplies—plus enough operating capital to get you through the first six months—you will probably need in excess of $30,000. Again, you can start the business for much less, but in doing so, you limit your growth potential—maybe even your ability to survive.

If you master the basics, though, you can make a profitable living in pest control. Learn as much as possible about the business, maintain high standards, and build your client base steadily, and this industry will make room for you.

=============== BRIGHT IDEA ===============

GOLF BALL GOFER

Admittedly, it isn't the business for everyone. But Orlando, Florida, entrepreneur Jim Reid has found his pot of gold at the bottom of golf-course ponds. Reid's Second Chance golf ball retrieval and recycling company specializes in underwater rescues—and turns a healthy profit for its trouble.

Reid learned to dive in Lake Texoma near his hometown of Kingston, Oklahoma. In the early 1970s, Reid headed to Florida in search of sunken treasure in shipwrecks. He never did see any gold doubloons, so he took a tip from a golf-pro acquaintance who asked him to dive into what he thought was a bottomless water hazard.

The result? "White gold! The bottom was covered with golf balls," says Reid. With the help of a self-designed washing machine and a secret chemical formula, which removes stains and algae, Reid sells the "nearly new" golf balls for up to 60 cents each. And nine years into the business, Reid recovered, cleaned, and repainted more than 5 million golf balls in 1989. With sales that approached $1 million in 1988 and twenty-two employees working almost twenty-four hours a day, it's no wonder golf-course supervisors are sending tons of golf balls to be sorted and graded for resale.

CURB-PAINTING SERVICE

High Net Profit Before Taxes:	$30,000
Average Net Profit Before Taxes:	$15,000
Minimum Start-up:	$7,000
Average Start-up:	$10,000

Thousands of people die at home each year from medical emergencies because the ambulance driver can't find the house. One reason is that many single-family homes don't have their street numbers visibly displayed. This is not only dangerous in the case of an emergency, but inconvenient for first-time visitors.

Hence, the need for curb-painting services. For a minimal fee—maybe $5 per address—a curb-painting service stencils house numbers on roadside curbs. The set-up couldn't be simpler: a few gallons of paint, a set of stencils, a few brushes, and you're in business. Low prices make for easy sales, and small jobs add up. A typical curb-painting operation can do eight jobs an hour, including transit time. Put in a six-hour day, and you can conceivably clear over $200.

Whose Curb Is It?

Though regulations vary from city to city (and you should check yours before you get started), as a rule, the maintenance and repair of curbs is controlled by city zoning or building inspection offices. In our research, we were unable to find any cities that prohibit independent contractors from establishing curb-painting services. You will, however, need to meet any requirements set for obtaining a business license.

Technically, it's up to the individual homeowner to post his or her house number on the curb. Therefore, it's up to you to convince homeowners that your service is worthy. Stress the safety and convenience factors, as well as your reasonable price. Also, make an extra effort to look professional. If you don't, chances are good no one will open their doors to hear your sales pitch.

Clearly, any homeowner with a home and a curb is a candidate for your service, but a little selectivity will boost your sales. Look for middle- to upper-middle-class neighborhoods where residents have the interest and money to pay for your service. Naturally, you'll want to eliminate any neighborhoods in which curbs are already neatly and recently painted. Businesses may also be good prospects for your service.

Ideal for Part-Time

Most curb-painting services go door-to-door pitching their services. If you work alone, you might choose to canvass in the morning and paint in the afternoon. Or consider working with a partner or employee: One of you can sell while the other paints.

Curb-painting makes an ideal part-time venture. You can bring in $200 to $500 on the weekends (when homeowners are generally home anyway) and keep your regular job. Some services take on the business full-time. Under ideal circumstances, it is possible to gross $30,000 a year working twenty-five hours a week. You may also supplement your income by offering adjunct services like housepainting, window washing, gardening, and so on.

HOME INSPECTION SERVICE

High Net Profit Before Taxes:	$105,000
Average Net Profit Before Taxes:	$60,000
Minimum Start-up:	$7,000
Average Start-up:	$18,450

Do you know a good home when you see one? Are you knowledgeable about construction, plumbing, and electrical systems? Are you thorough, detail-oriented, even picky? You may have what it takes to start a home inspection service.

The home inspection industry has experienced tremendous growth over the past decade. According to the American Society of Home Inspectors (ASHI), only 2 percent of the homes sold in the early 1980s were inspected by professionals. In 1989, over 30 percent were inspected, and that number is expected to double by the mid-1990s. And as the industry grows, the number of qualified independent home inspectors will grow with it.

A Matter of Common Sense

When you consider the role of a professional home inspector in the buying process, you may wonder why inspectors haven't been standard fixtures all along. That home buyers would want an expert opinion before buying a home is only common sense. With housing prices at an all-time high, the stakes are higher than ever. After all, who wants a $300,000 lemon?

A home inspector examines the house's interior, exterior, roof, pavement, foundation, siding, electrical systems, plumbing, heating-cooling systems, attic, and basement, then reports his or her findings to the potential buyers. In some cases, flaws uncovered by an inspector result in a lower selling price. In other instances, buyers withdraw their offers altogether. Occasionally, a home even gets a clean bill of health—and buyers, in turn, get a clean conscience.

The ideal client for a home inspection service is an experienced home buyer who is buying a home five to ten years old. Experienced buyers know the kinds of troubles (and expenses) that can arise from a problem-plagued house, and are more than willing to fork over $250 or more for a good evaluation. This isn't to say that first-time home buyers aren't a good target market. They are, and so are real-estate agents, who are eager to offer this additional service to their clients. Real-estate agents get the added benefit of transferring liability for future problems from themselves to the inspector.

Know Thy Business

Liability is an important issue in home inspection. When you inspect a home, you promise to spot any potential problems. If you are negligent or incompetent, you may be liable for expenses resulting from an unreported problem.

In other words, this is no business for know-nothings. While it's possible to break into this field with just a passing knowledge of construction and electrical work, sloppy inspection doesn't pay. Take the time to develop real expertise. Most successful inspectors have extensive backgrounds in construction, architecture, engineering, or general contracting.

With the proper qualifications and experience, home inspection can be a lucrative and growing business. Start-up costs are low—as little as $7,000 if you work from home. The tools of the home inspection trade are many. Some are as basic as ladders, flashlights, binoculars, screwdrivers, and coveralls. More sophisticated equipment includes radon testing kits, voltage testers, tick tracers, moisture meters, and water testing kits. Don't skimp on the essentials. Good tools are a wise business investment.

An established, reliable home inspector can make an enviable income. We estimate high net profits at over $100,000. With strong salesmanship, a healthy market, and a team of inspectors, there is virtually no limit to growth in this business.

=============== BRIGHT IDEA ===============

TRAVEL TRAINING

America's travel and tourism industry is booming. But to break into most travel businesses, applicants need training. Where do they get it?

One place is Echols Travel and Hotel Schools, Chicago-based travel and tourism training centers. Echols has trained over 12,000 students in the Chicago area alone for careers with major hotels, airlines, cruise lines, and travel agencies. The curricula include classes on operating airline and hotel computers, running tours, planning meetings, and marketing travel packages.

Company founder Evelyn Echols started the school twenty-eight years ago. Today, she's expanding her company through licensing. Echols trains licensees on starting and marketing a travel school and offers ongoing assistance on a fee basis.

POOL CLEANING AND REPAIR

High Net Profit Before Taxes:	$170,000
Average Net Profit Before Taxes:	$62,000
Minimum Start-up:	$9,600
Average Start-up:	$21,600

We admit this isn't the business to start in Alaska. But in
many American communities, swimming pools are a common amenity. In fact, there are currently more than 4 million
swimming pools in the United States. And each one has to be
cleaned, maintained, and repaired. The pool construction,
products, and aftermarket sales represent a $4.7 billion in-
dustry—one that's expected to grow substantially in the
years to come.

Making a Splash

Though it does require expertise, the pool repair and
maintenance business is fairly easy to learn. Better still, it is
easy to get into for a small investment. If you have a truck or
van, some brushes, hoses, nets, a vacuum, a testing kit, an
initial supply of chemicals, and a few additional tools for
repair work, you're ready to get started. The average cash
investment for a new service is only $21,600; the average net
profit is $62,000—not a bad living by anyone's standards.

One area of expertise you'll need to develop is water chemistry, or maintaining the proper balance of chemicals in the
pool water. Learning water chemistry takes some time, but
information is readily available through chemical dealers
and the National Spa and Pool Institute in Alexandria, Virginia. In addition to testing the water, pool services clear
pools of leaves, dirt, and other debris. This work is as simple
as running a net through the water.

The second biggest challenge in starting a pool service is
establishing a route. Perhaps the easiest way to do this is to
buy a route from an existing service. If this isn't an option,
going door-to-door, distributing flyers, or sending brochures
through the mail are effective, economical tactics. Building a
client base from scratch can take time, so plan accordingly.
You may opt to stay in your regular job until your business is
up and running. You can easily service a few accounts on
weekends and off-hours.

'Tis the Season

Pool services are not always year-round businesses. In
California, Hawaii, Arizona, Texas, and Florida, the weather

permits year-round use, but in most other parts of the country, pools are drained and shut down in the winter.

Before you launch your pool service, try to determine the patterns of use in your area. Year-round users represent a steadier market. In warmer climates, you can expect to service forty to sixty pools a month for a regular income. Where winter shuts pools down, much of your business will be opening pools in the summer and closing them in the winter. While seasonal users also contract for weekly service, they are less likely to do so than year-round clients.

If your business is likely to be seasonal, make plans for January through March, when business will come to a halt. You may want to consider a seasonal winter business like Christmas tree sales or snowplowing. Or you may want to budget your income so that those three months are an extended vacation—not a bad option if you can swing it.

SELF-SERVICE STORAGE

High Net Profit Before Taxes:	$95,000-plus
Average Net Profit Before Taxes:	$60,000
Minimum Start-up:	$41,000
Average Start-up:	$150,000

Wherever you live, wherever you work, you probably need more space. And you aren't the only one. Just about everyone suffers from a shortage of storage space at one time or another. Many of these sufferers turn to the nation's 10,000 self-service storage facilities to ease the burden.

Old Concept, New Twist

There's nothing new about storing goods. But the approach taken by self-service storage facilities is relatively recent. During the 1970s, mini-warehouses began popping up around the country. They made warehousing accessible to small businesses and individuals who couldn't afford—or wouldn't think of—conventional warehouse space.

The point is, only businesses need warehousing. But just about everyone needs a little extra space. Whether they're college students going home for the summer, apartment dwellers between leases, or professionals with acres of outdated files, storage customers appreciate the convenience, privacy, and affordability of self-service storage.

Assess Your Market

Twenty years ago, you could open a storage facility just about anywhere and expect to make a profit. Today, increased competition makes market research a must. Consider such factors as local economic conditions, housing standards, and business vs. residential occupancy. Also investigate other facilities in your area. How will you compete?

Another change that's taken place in this industry: Marketing is no longer an option, but a necessity. Set aside a healthy portion of your start-up money for advertising and promotion, and work out a continuing ad program once the business is established. The demand for self-service storage facilities continues unabated. Your task is to beat out the competition for the demand that exists.

5

COMPUTER BUSINESSES

COMPUTER HARDWARE STORE

High Net Profit Before Taxes:	$86,000
Average Net Profit Before Taxes:	$55,000
Minimum Start-up:	$45,000
Average Start-up:	$70,000

Sales of computers in the United States are roughly $32 billion annually. As the 1980s began, we scoffed at—and even feared—the introduction of the personal computer. Now, many of us can't function without them. Whether for business or pleasure, at the office, in the den or the dorm room, computers are here to stay. And so, we're happy to report, are the stores that sell them.

More Affordable by the Day

In 1960, it took a roomful of equipment worth $3 million to accomplish what one desktop computer can do today for $2,500 or less. No wonder we're so infatuated with our computers: Thanks to advancing technology, the average person is able to harness computer power he or she could only dream of thirty years ago.

While relatively low prices make computers accessible to consumers, the hottest and largest small-computer market is small business. Many small businesses spend from $6,000 to $10,000 and more to computerize their companies. For them, increased efficiency makes even large computer expenditures wise investments.

Better still, the rapidly expanding software industry makes computers more and more useful every day. Today, there is software for every conceivable activity—from word processing and accounting to robot design and wedding planning. Not only are computers essential in most businesses, but they are also becoming indispensable in just about every department within those businesses.

What You'll Sell

The two main components of a personal computer are the hardware and the software. Hardware retailers usually stock a few basic software programs, but the focus is decidedly on hardware. Therefore, some of the items you will sell include central processing units, keyboards, monitors, modems, printers, cables, and an assortment of minor accessories, supplies, handbooks, and tools. Typically, a computer retailer will limit the number of lines he or she carries so as to focus on selling a few effectively.

In addition to products, most computer stores sell limited but necessary services. One is repairs and maintenance. Some computer retailers offer in-house repairs, others send off defective components to the manufacturer on behalf of their customers. Besides repairs, some service-oriented shops offer classes in basic programming and use. Customers appreciate this extra service and the classroom setting is excellent for explaining the merits of your various products.

In today's computer market, it is critical to keep up with the industry. Advances are made daily in this volatile business. While that means increased sales potential for you, it also means that you must pay attention to new trends and products. Staying informed about your merchandise—and your market—will spell the difference between mediocre sales and success.

COMPUTER REPAIR BUSINESS

High Net Profit Before Taxes:	$30,000
Average Net Profit Before Taxes:	$23,000
Minimum Start-up:	$17,000
Average Start-up:	$24,000

Like everything else, computers break. And when they do, they can immobilize a business. Those of us who spend our lives in front of a monitor literally cannot function without our computers.

And that spells good news for the computer repair industry. In the past decade, computers have become common fixtures in businesses and at home. Anyone who uses a computer regularly can tell you that they aren't maintenance-free. Not only do they require regular cleaning and troubleshooting, but they also need occasional repairs. Master the science of computer repair and you'll find a ready market for your services. Can't tell a screwdriver from a disk drive? You can still break into this growing business by hiring a technician and handling sales and customer service yourself.

Convenience Is Key

Computer repair services are not the only sources of repair. In fact, most hardware retailers offer service after the sale. And while the computer is warrantied, hardware can be returned to the manufacturer for service. What a computer repair service offers that these other outlets don't is convenience. Most users rely totally on their computers to get their work done. And most will pay a higher price to get their computers picked up, fixed, and returned in a hurry.

Computer repair services speed repairs by replacing defective components instead of tinkering with them. Say, for example, that a client's disk drive is acting up. Once you isolate the problem, you simply replace the drive with a new one in stock. This process, known as pure assembly exchange, saves you time and headaches. Better yet, you can

return the client's computer in a day, saving him or her time
and headaches, too.

Many computer repair services rent storefronts near
other computer businesses. This way, they attract walk-in
customers in addition to regular clients. But if you're operating on a shoestring, you might also consider working from a
home or studio. By emphasizing pick-up and delivery and
marketing your service aggressively, you can still build a
good client base and avoid the expense of renting a fancy
location.

=========== BRIGHT IDEA ===========

PIXEL PERFECT

At some time or another, almost every homeowner wants to
remodel some portion of the house or yard. For Howard
Lefkowitz, this desire sparked a business—computer imaging.

When Lefkowitz, now president of Visual Translations
Inc. in Woodland Hills, California, had his own home remodeled, he remembers, "I kept asking someone to show me
what it would look like, and nobody ever did." That's when he
set out to develop a computer-imaging software package.

While designer's watercolor renderings and blueprints offer some idea of what remodeling will look like, most homeowners are somewhat uncertain about the ultimate results.

Now, thanks to computer-imaging technology that enables computers to show "before and after" images on a video
screen, home and commercial remodelers can finally see the
finished product before they even start. And customers at
Visual Translations are willing to pay for it. Consumers are
paying between $150 and $350 to see their homes transformed before their eyes, and commercial remodelers are
shelling out at least $700 to see their buildings take on a new
look.

Since founding Visual Translations in 1988, Lefkowitz
has helped hundreds of remodelers visualize results in advance. And although Visual Translations is one of a handful

of computer companies offering computer imaging, Lefkowitz expects to see several more computer-imaging companies emerge soon. Since homeowners spend billions of dollars on remodeling each year, the market for this service will undoubtedly continue to grow.

SOFTWARE RETAILING

High Net Profit Before Taxes:	$105,000
Average Net Profit Before Taxes:	$45,000
Minimum Start-up:	$53,000
Average Start-up:	$70,000

The computer industry is constantly changing, and nowhere so fast as in the software business. The nation's software manufacturers continually introduce new programs and revise existing ones. Moreover, users' needs change. As more and more powerful programs become available, the urge to upgrade takes over. Even people with libraries of software occasionally find themselves in the market for a new program.

The trend in software retailing is toward stores that sell only software (and perhaps a few accessories). Hardware retailers continue to sell software, but usually with a reduced selection and without customer service support. Serious software buyers usually look for a specialized software store—and that's where you, the aspiring retailer, come in.

Booting Up

A typical software store costs $50,000 to $75,000 to start up. Square footage starts at 800 to 1,000 square feet and tops out at about 1,500 square feet. Look for a space in a shopping district or small center: A mall location will probably be needlessly expensive for this type of store. About 70 percent of your start-up cost is inventory, so establishing credit with major software manufacturers should be a priority.

You do not need to be a technical wizard to start a software store, but you should be familiar with different types of software, their uses, and general customer needs. You should also have technical assistance available for customers when they need it. Service and support are major factors in bringing customers back to an independent software shop.

The Software Market

One of the largest markets for PC software consists of entertainment software, particularly games. Educational software is also popular among young parents who hope to get their brood off to a technically competent start. These types of programs appeal mainly to young, college-educated professionals who have discretionary income to spend on computer gadgets.

Businesses are also a prime market for software stores. Word processing, spreadsheet, and database programs are among the most popular in this category, and choices abound. Smart software retailers know their merchandise well enough to assess a buyer's needs, recommend an appropriate program, and provide follow-up support. To do this, you will have to bone up—and so will your salespeople. Another tip: Speak plain English. For most businesspeople, computerese is a turnoff, while plain English is such a rarity that you may make a sale on that basis alone.

Most software stores also cater to computer buffs. Yet, according to industry experts, this share of the market is shrinking as a proportion of the total business. The future of the industry seems to be in consumer sales, not sales to esoteric whiz-types. To that end, keep your approach accessible. The average software buyer needs basic information and service. Stress that, and your software store will be off to a good start.

========= BRIGHT IDEA =========

SPECIALTY SOFTWARE

Jim and Sheri Standen were overwhelmed when planning their wedding in 1989, so to get organized, they developed

The Personal Computer Wedding Planner, a software program designed to make some sense of prewedding confusion.

Since then, the software has evolved into a full-time business called Auscan Data Services. "After we used the Wedding Planner for ourselves, we realized how useful it would be for other couples and wedding coordinators," says Sheri, "so I quit my job to market the product full time."

The Standens aren't the only ones who have used customized software to solve knotty problems. Around the country, clever programmers are creating software to fit particular needs. In New Jersey, a nurse helped develop software especially designed for nurses. Similar programs have been developed for small-business accounting, term-paper formatting, and order processing, to name just a few functions.

To get into the software development business, programming ability is a major plus. But it is possible to hire that expertise if, for example, you have firsthand knowledge of what the market wants. Remember too that good programming isn't the only factor in success. You'll need excellent marketing and support to make your program a hit.

SOFTWARE SEARCH SERVICE

High Net Profit Before Taxes:	$91,000
Average Net Profit Before Taxes:	$45,000
Minimum Start-up:	$19,000
Average Start-up:	$25,000

With more than 100,000 software programs available on the market, the search for the right software grows more difficult each day. Programs come and go at the drop of a hat. And the technology is improving so rapidly that it's hard to keep pace. Increasingly, the task is beyond the scope of the average buyer—or even professional computer consultants and retailers. Instead of agonizing over the decision, those in the know have software search firms aid in the shopping process.

What Is a Search Service?

A software search service maintains a database listing of available programs, cross-referenced under several categories (for instance, IBM vs. Macintosh or spreadsheet vs. word processing). Clients or subscribers call you with their specifications. You punch the information into your own data bank, and out pops a list of software on the market that is most likely to fit their needs.

How does this service differ from retail sales or catalogs? Your list will be more comprehensive than a retailer's selection and more up-to-date than the average catalog's. You can offer a more accurate picture of a program's capabilities than catalog listings do. And your opinion is objective, since you don't profit by pushing the most expensive program.

Many Markets to Tap

Most of your clients will be businesses. They need programs to handle specific functions and will call on you to steer them in the right direction. Business clients include both first-time computer users and current computer users looking to expand their capabilities.

In addition to business clients, you may serve computer professionals. Often consultants, programmers, and retailers are faced with finding the right program for their clients. When they draw a blank—or want a comprehensive list of alternatives—they frequently call software search services for advice. For them, locating the right program can mean the difference between closing the sale and losing it.

Start on a Budget

Breaking into the software search business isn't expensive if you manage your money wisely. Your main expenses will be a computer to hold the database, a telephone, stationery, and advertising. If you hire outside help to input data, that too will be an expense. But you can save money by entering the data yourself—possibly in the evenings and on weekends before you start the service. An average investment of $25,000 should put you in business.

Returns on your investment can be handsome. Average net pretax profits are in the $40,000 to $50,000 range, and six-figure profits are not out of the question. The trick is providing quality information on the spot. Maintain high standards for accuracy and currency, market your service well, and a software search service could be your ticket to entrepreneurship.

===================== BRIGHT IDEA =====================

TONER CARTRIDGE RECHARGING

The computer industry is gaining momentum in the business world every second, and the laser printer toner cartridge recharging industry is clearly along for the ride.

"Approximately 100,000 laser printers are presently being sold in the United States per month," says Les Paull, president of Austin, Texas-based LaserCharge Inc. "In order to print, each of those machines needs a cartridge. We recharge toner cartridges for a fraction of what it would cost to buy a new one."

Laser cartridge recharging businesses remove the cartridges from the printers, check the movable parts, replace the parts if necessary, and then replenish the toner to make the cartridge reusable. Individuals can break into the recharging business by either acquiring licenses from recharging companies for an average of $5,000 to $7,000, or by establishing the business independently.

The return on investment is great either way, according to Paull. "A cartridge costs a dealer about $12 to $13 to recharge, and they typically turn around and sell the cartridges to the consumer for between $39 and $60," he says. "Considering that a good recharger can do four to eight cartridges per hour, that's a lot of money."

For entrepreneurs interested in setting up a home-based business, toner cartridge recharging is an ideal opportunity because a storefront isn't a prerequisite. Rechargers pull initial clientele from mailing lists of new cartridge buyers and advertising, and they build their own businesses from there.

COMPUTER CONSULTING AND TEMPORARY HELP SERVICE

High Net Profit Before Taxes:	$150,000-plus
Average Net Profit Before Taxes:	$80,000
Minimum Start-up:	$23,000
Average Start-up:	$45,000

Everybody and his brother has a computer today, but do they know how to use it? According to BIS CAP International, a marketing research and consulting firm in Norwell, Massachusetts, more than 7.1 million personal computers were sold in 1988, and that figure is expected to climb to almost 8 million this year. Many of these purchasers are confused, first-time users who need assistance from a computer consultant.

Computer consulting is a low-investment business that can be operated from home, and can work well on a part-time basis. Just $9,000 was enough to get Michael Wilding and Paul Goldner started in their New York City company, Micro-Trek. So far, the partners have trained more than 150,000 members of the business community. MicroTrek's services also include computer programming, networking, accounting systems, and financial modeling. After six years in business, the pair—who describe themselves as "businessmen, not techies"—oversee forty employees and have gross billings of more than $3 million.

The Learning Lag

Almost no one disputes the usefulness of computers in today's business world. But not everyone understands how to use them. Sometimes total ignorance rules. Believe it or not, there are still people who don't know a floppy disk from a CD. In other cases, new technology presents new challenges.

In any case, computer ignorance costs money. For every day workers spend figuring out a new system, the company loses valuable production time. Thus, it pays to hire an expert to get a new system up and running—and to bring employees up to snuff. Even at $40 to $90 an hour, a computer consultant can be worth his or her weight in gold.

Similarly, companies need temporary workers to fill technical slots. When they're shorthanded—or when a special project arises—hiring a qualified temp can be cheaper than retraining an existing employee or slowing production.

Down to Business

What does this mean for you, the aspiring entrepreneur? You can match consultants and temporary workers with companies who need their expertise. In return, you profit by marking up their services. Suppose the going rate for a data entry person is $10 an hour. You can charge clients $18 an hour for the convenience of getting a qualified worker on the spot, and keep the $8-an-hour difference for your trouble. Higher-paid consultants bring in an even higher markup.

There are three main elements to a successful computer consulting firm. They are:
1) Strong recruitment and screening abilities,
2) Accurate accounting and billing procedures, and
3) A vigorous approach to marketing.

On paper, these sound easy. But in practice, they can be tricky. Your success hinges on your ability to bring in topflight consultants and workers. Clients can hire incompetent help on their own. You don't have to be a computer genius to make it in this business, but you should know enough about computers to evaluate a candidate's competence.

You should also know enough about business and marketing to keep operations running smoothly. Remember that you don't have to do it all: Few successful consulting companies are one-person operations. Where you lack experience, hire help. The professional results will boost your business image and ultimately improve the bottom line.

6

RETAIL

PRINT AND POSTER SHOP

High Net Profit Before Taxes:	$120,000
Average Net Profit Before Taxes:	$67,000
Minimum Start-up:	$17,000
Average Start-up:	$47,000

From Rambo to Renoir, Americans are plastering their walls and halls with posters and prints. The incredible variety means that posters can be found to match anyone's taste. The affordability of posters is the key to attracting starving college students; it also lets corporate executives impress clients with sharply framed prints without blowing the budget on originals.

Making It in Print

The affordably priced poster has been evolving ever since the turn of the century, when the popularity of theater created a need for posters to advertise plays and vaudeville acts. During World War I, posters became part of the war effort, chiding the public to buy war bonds or join the service. Later, the movie industry used posters to acclaim the stars of the silver screen, and political campaigns plastered the names of their candidates across poster board.

It was the flower children of the late 1960s and early

1970s who gave poster sales their biggest boost. The craze picked up momentum as teenagers and rock music fans collected the "black light" impressions of Jimi Hendrix, Janis Joplin, and other stars, along with various psychedelic, neon-colored, glow-in-the-dark pop art posters. Again, the key to posters' popularity was their low price.

The enormous popularity of rock posters spilled over to other categories. Poster aficionados could choose among pictures of movie personalities, sports celebrities, nature scenes, wildlife shots, Oriental themes, and that catch-all category, contemporary art. Soon, artists discovered that there was an overwhelmingly large consumer market for limited editions and high-quality poster reproductions of original works. The general public, and particularly college students, were willing to pay $25 to $50 for a sharp reproduction on slick poster board.

Today, the $5 billion poster and print art industry offers a huge variety of posters and prints with a wide spectrum of price tags. However, the prices can be roughly segmented: inexpensive (less than $10), midrange ($10 to $99), and numbered limited editions ($100 and more). Limited edition posters usually number 2,000. Limited edition numbered prints are typically distributed in a block of only 250.

Location Is Key

Shopping malls are the location of choice for most franchised print and poster shops. Heavy foot traffic keeps these galleries visible. It's also essential to maintain eye-catching displays of framed prints and posters.

After location, the second biggest factor in the success of a print and poster shop is selection. Staying abreast of industry trends and customer tastes is critical to keeping your business ahead of the pack. In today's traditional market, museum prints are selling well. But the market changes constantly, and smart retailers know how to keep in touch with the market.

Part of that equation is knowing who your customers are. Do you bring in a lot of college students? Are many of your clients corporate (remember, providing prints for an entire office building can make your whole month)? Does your store attract affluent homeowners, looking for the latest colors and styles? Chances are, your market will consist of all these groups, but one may predominate. Get to know your customers and find out what they like.

To Frame or Not to Frame?

One way or another, you will probably offer framing services to your customers. The question is, will you provide these services yourself or contract them out to a local frame shop?

Some operators limit their framing services to mounting, an inexpensive method of attaching the poster to corrugated cardboard with a plastic covering bordered by metallic tape and a sturdy cardboard hook on the back. This form of framing is fine with teenagers and poor college students, but often not sophisticated enough for adults.

If you decide to launch your own framing operation, be warned that framing is not simple. Like any craft, poster framing is a labor of love and patience. Professional training is available under the guidance of the Professional Picture Framers Association in Richmond, Virginia. You can, however, bring in additional profits with framing services. Industry experts estimate that framing services can double a shop's gross sales—a good reason to invest time and money in learning the craft.

The Chop Shop

Another compromise between offering no framing and full service is the "chop service" arrangement. An assortment of colored wood and metal frames is available in the poster shop, and customers can select the molding of their choice. The shop owner then calls in the frame order over the telephone to a "chop shop," which cuts the molding to custom specifications and ships it to the poster store within 24 to 48 hours.

Using a chop shop enables the poster shop owner to eliminate the space needed for producing frames and the additional space needed to store the frame inventory. In some cases, chop shops are a necessity, since local ordinances may prohibit so-called light manufacturing in a mall or shopping center location.

=== BRIGHT IDEA ===

PEDDLING PETALS

When Ellen Galeki spotted a mobile flower shop in her neighborhood, she was impressed with the concept—so impressed, in fact, that she ended up buying it. "The Flower Concierge used to come to my neighborhood all the time," she says. "It was very popular, too. People used to flock to the truck every time it arrived. But one day, the truck just stopped coming to my area. When I called to ask why they weren't coming anymore, the former owners said they were going out of business. 'No, you're not!' I said. 'I'm going to buy you out.'"

Galeki stuck to her word. She bought the business in January of 1989, and became operational in March. Today, she's operating the Flower Concierge with what she describes as a personalized approach. "The men I bought the business from never actually worked out of the truck, but I am involved in every aspect of the business—from selling on the truck to ordering the flowers—and I know what my customers want," says Galeki.

The Flower Concierge specializes in three areas: flowers for offices, flowers for residences, and special occasions like weddings and parties. Sales aren't the only emphasis at the Flower Concierge; service is also stressed. "I employ a floral designer who does the individual arrangements, and I use my own art degree and eye for interior design to place the flowers strategically in each location according to the customer's desires," says Galeki. "The finishing touches really make a difference."

Galeki's customers, primarily wealthy residents of Los Angeles' Westside, understand the importance of the added touch her imported and exotic flowers provide. Best of all, that extra service doesn't cost the customer more. Because Galeki's overhead is relatively low, her prices are reasonable. In fact, she's sometimes even cheaper than retail.

OFF-PRICE RETAILING

High Net Profit Before Taxes:	$755,000
Average Net Profit Before Taxes:	$311,000
Minimum Start-up:	$128,000
Average Start-up:	$300,000

Anyone who's visited a department store of late knows how outrageous retail prices have become. A pair of jeans are a "bargain" at $50; cotton baby sleepers run as high as $40. And that doesn't account for "designer" prices on careerwear, eveningwear, and even housewares like sheets and towels.

With prices soaring, it's no wonder that consumers are sounding the cry, "Never pay retail." Discount shopping isn't just for the down market anymore. More and more upscale shoppers are resolving never to pay retail. And consequently, off-price retailing has experienced an incredible upsurge in growth.

Off-Price, On Target

Just what is an off-price retailer? Technically speaking, an off-price retailer is anyone who sells merchandise for less than the suggested retail price. A retailer can lower the retail price either by reducing the markup or by purchasing inventory for reduced prices. Liquidators, flea-market vendors, factory outlets, discount chains, membership warehouses, and closeout stores are all off-price outlets.

But perhaps the fastest-growing segment of the off-price market is the upscale discounter. These retailers don't sell off-brands; they sell designer or name-brand product lines. This sets them apart from traditional discount stores like K-Mart, or flea-market vendors with anonymous merchandise. The merchandise at today's off-price outlets isn't likely to be distressed, either. Rather, the goods are high-quality close-outs and overstock items that sell for as much as 60 percent less than they would in a department store. The merchandise may be priced for the down market, but it's packaged for the upscale shopper.

Sudden Impact

Off-price retailing has grown steadily since it was first introduced about twenty-five years ago. But only in the last ten years have off-price retailers really made their presence felt throughout the retailing industry. During the recession of the 1970s, consumers considered off-price outlets a boon—they were the only place most people could afford brand-name goods. The 1970s ended, but the trend toward off-price shopping did not. Between 1983 and 1986, off-price sales rose 66 percent, from $6.9 billion to $11.5 billion.

Though some industry insiders predict a leveling off in the next few years, they don't deny that there's still room for growth in off-price retailing. One strategy is to develop a specialty. In Chicago, one off-price men's apparel retailer brings in sales of $1,000 per square foot (compared to $124 for a department store and $200 for a typical off-pricer). His secret? Low prices and exceptional service—two things that are hard to come by in a department store. After more than twenty years in business, his reputation speaks for itself.

Shrewd-Shopping Owners

The market for off-price retailers looks good in the years to come. But before you quit your job to start an off-price outlet, be forewarned that this isn't a cheap business to get into. Based on our research, the minimum investment for this type of business is $133,000. A more average figure is $300,000. You can get started for less if you specialize in one area—for instance, men's apparel or children's clothing. But even then, your minimum investment won't be small. Putting together the right inventory in a good location costs money.

On the other hand, you will spend less stocking an off-price outlet than you would setting up a comparably sized department store. For this, you must be a shopper extraordinaire. Opportunistic buying is the key to off-price profits.

Manufacturer's overstocks, irregular (but saleable) goods, odd lots, discontinued items, and liquidated goods are just a few sources that off-price retailers tap. Establishing contacts and learning what to buy are of primary importance to the off-price retailer.

The Competition's Hot

As more and more players get into the off-price game, the competition is heating up. Successful off-pricers already exist—and they're a smart bunch. To get into the business now, you must be a savvy buyer and a hard worker. You must also have enough capital to set up, stock, and promote your business adequately. At the same time, potential profits are high—as high as $755,000, according to our estimates. With the right planning and management, though, you can make high profits from low prices.

CHILDREN'S BOOKSTORE

High Net Profit Before Taxes:	$45,000
Average Net Profit Before Taxes:	$30,000
Minimum Start-up:	$23,000
Average Start-up:	$85,000

Experts have long touted the benefits of reading to very young children. Some parents even start reading to their children before they are born! With today's well-educated baby boomers anxious to give their children a good start in life, it's no wonder that children's bookstores are experiencing a major surge in popularity and profits.

According to the Center for Book Research at the University of Scranton, children's bookstores are leading the publishing industry in annual dollar sale increases. Juvenile paperbacks had the best dollar growth increases, while juvenile hardbacks had the best annual unit gains.

In the coming decade, the demand for children's books will continue to increase, according to J. Kendrick Noble, a publishing analyst for PaineWebber in New York City. "The boom will continue for up to ten years," Noble says, "because most children's books are bought for 6- to 12-year-olds."

A Knee-High View

Most regular bookstores carry children's books, but children's bookstores go the extra mile to encourage youngsters to read. Many offer "storytelling hours," where children meet in small groups to hear books read aloud. The selection is wide and varied, the decor is youthful, and the staff is helpful. The bookstore as a whole is designed to appeal to kids— and, in turn, to their parents.

Industry insiders say this is the ideal business for children's book lovers. They say this because, in order to succeed, you will have to read a lot of children's books. Parents will frequent your store on the assumption that you are more helpful and knowledgeable than a general bookstore clerk. In addition to scanning titles, a good children's bookseller will stay in close touch with vendors, and attend plenty of seminars, conventions, and trade shows.

Profit margins on books are tight. A 40 percent markup is standard. To increase sales and profits, many children's bookstores also stock related items: toys, audio and video tapes, etc. This concept works fine, as long as your auxiliary merchandise doesn't overpower the books you're in business to sell.

Hands-on Business

With the recent baby boomlet and rekindled interest in literacy, children's bookstores are an excellent risk in the current marketplace. However, they are not usually big-money operations. According to our sources, a $45,000 net profit is high for this industry, and $30,000 is probably more realistic.

What's more, this is not an absentee business. While you may be able to hire an enthusiastic and knowledgeable manager to run the business for you, doing so defeats the purpose of starting a children's bookstore. If you want an absentee operation, insiders agree, look for another business. Children's bookstores are most successful when run by eager, dedicated owners.

═══════════════════ BRIGHT IDEA ═══════════════════

NEWS ON THE RUN

"I'd like a *Wall Street Journal* and a decaf, please." So go the orders at the Press Box News Drive-Thru Newsstand. The latest in drive-thru concepts, Press Box News sells everything you could possibly want on your morning drive to work: newspapers, magazines, coffee, sodas, juice, cigarettes, lottery tickets, snacks, and film processing. All this in a diminutive package—only 100 square feet.

The Press Box News is the brainchild of Scott A. Blitz and Ken A. Beck, two Lancaster, Pennsylvania, entrepreneurs who hope to see Press Box News kiosks around the country soon. Blitz and Beck spent three years conducting research before launching the first Press Box News Drive-Thru in Ephrata, Pennsylvania, in 1985.

They now have six operating franchises and are committed to sixty-five more. During peak hours, from six A.M. to ten A.M., about seventy customers zoom through each newsstand each hour. "Most people are off the freeway, through the drive-thru, and back on the freeway in about one minute," says Beck. This convenience is proving profitable: Beck says some units are grossing close to $400,000 a year.

SILK PLANT SHOP

High Net Profit Before Taxes:	$105,456
Average Net Profit Before Taxes:	$58,860
Minimum Start-up:	$5,167
Average Start-up:	$24,200

A few years back, a pair of wisecracking entrepreneurs introduced the Everbrown, a houseplant that required no care because—frankly—it was dead. The concept was funny, but it wasn't necessarily unique. Many of us have grown our own "Everbrowns" through neglect and ignorance.

At work and at home, many consumers don't have the

time or the expertise to grow their own plants. Yet most still enjoy having plants around. As an alternative to troublesome live plants, more and more people are beginning to decorate with artificial silk plants. The market for maintenance-free greenery has opened up new opportunities for entrepreneurs across the country. In this plant business, a green thumb is not required.

Silk Makes the Difference

Not long ago, the majority of artificial plants were made from plastic and looked cheap and phony. In recent years, however, the quality of artificial plants has improved tremendously. Today, artificial plants often look so real that unless you touch a leaf or try to smell a flower, you won't realize they aren't the real thing.

Although the industry refers to these realistic knock-offs as "silk plants," some are not made of silk at all. Cotton, linen, polyester, and velvet are also used. Today's fakes are a far cry from the plastic variety of the sixties. Manufacturers make a concerted effort to replicate nature. Not only are leaves believable, but stems are hand-wrapped to look authentic. The result is a product that even the most upscale consumers can live with—something that the plastic plants of yesteryear certainly couldn't claim.

Design Your Own Business

The silk plant business offers a variety of opportunities to the new entrepreneur. You may opt to open a retail silk plant shop. Or you might decide to sell your arrangements wholesale to florists, furniture stores, and specialty shops. One entrepreneur we interviewed specializes in business accounts. She will design a veritable forest of trees, plants, and flowers for restaurants, offices, hotels, stores, and interior designers. If starting out slow appeals to you, consider making silk flowers at home and selling them through swap meets, crafts fairs, and home parties.

Home-based silk plant businesses can expect to bring in about $6,000 to $12,000 annually working part-time. Retail operations can gross as much as $200,000 to $300,000 a year, according to a franchisor we interviewed. Start-up costs vary from as little as $2,500 for a home-based venture, to about $50,000 for a full-service retail outlet.

Demand Is Heating Up

Silk plants promise to become even more popular in the years to come. High quality products and total adaptability (finally, customers can grow palms in Alaska!) make silk plants and flowers more and more appealing to consumers. And the trend feeding their popularity—lack of spare time at home and work—shows no sign of slowing down.

"SWEATS"-ONLY APPAREL

High Net Profit Before Taxes:	$180,000
Average Net Profit Before Taxes:	$40,000
Minimum Start-up:	$60,000
Average Start-up:	$85,000

Recently seen at some of the trendiest spots in the country: sweats. Yes, sweatshirts and sweatpants aren't just for sweating anymore. They've become the casual wear of choice for a nation that works hard and plays seriously.

These are not the mottled gray garments you dragged home from gym class in high school. Today's sweats come in a wide range of styles and colors—so many, in fact, that entire stores are devoted to them.

A Few Sizes Fit All

The sweats-only shop is not just fun for the consumer. Retailers rejoice as well, since sweats are a low-hassle, high-markup item. Sweats typically come in four sizes: small, medium, large, and extra large. Most of the population fits within these four parameters, as compared to six sizes of women's dresses or a dozen sizes of men's pants. Moreover, sweats don't fit like the perennial glove. They're supposed to be loose and comfortable, so exact fit isn't an issue.

Better still, a retailer can sell sweats for twice what he or she paid and still offer the consumer a low price. As the business grows and your volume increases, your buying power should lower wholesale prices even further, thus improving your profit margin.

Though many sweats-only stores sell plain goods only, you can expand your business to include silkscreening or hand-painting. One sweats-only chain in the Midwest does this, using art students from local colleges. Customizing adds $6 to $35 per item to gross revenues, and acts as an added attraction for the stores.

Make It Colorful

Though sweats appeal to a broad market, your target consumer is 18 to 35 years old. In choosing a location, look for areas with students, young professionals, and active families. Also pay special attention to your merchandising and displays. One sweats-only store we found stacks the goods on shelves by color, creating long columns of red, blue, purple, black, and so on for a fun effect.

Keep abreast of fashion trends as well. While sweats aren't a true fashion item, trendy colors and offbeat styles sell. Follow fashion trends, and look for manufacturers who offer interesting designs and colors. After all, part of your marketing statement is that sweats can be chic.

=========== BRIGHT IDEA ===========

PETITE SHOP

According to a report by the New York City-based market research firm FIND/SVP, $208.6 billion of the total $1.5 trillion generated in retail sales in 1986 was spent in specialty retail establishments. Among the hottest growth segments for specialty retailers: petite apparel.

The age-old notion that every woman is—or should be—one size is fading into obscurity. For years, petite women faced bleak fashion choices. Either they had to alter regular fashions to fit their frames, which was expensive and often had dubious results, or they bought teen clothing and looked "cute." Even though department stores have begun stocking petite clothes, the selection available in regular outlets is limited. Today's women need a variety of clothes for work and leisure. Why shouldn't a petite woman have as many choices as her regular-sized counterpart?

Running a petite shop isn't so different from operating a regular women's clothing boutique—only the sizes have been changed. As in any independent clothing store, the important factors to consider are style, selection, and service. Emphasize clothing that suits mature or upwardly mobile women, not adolescent fashions. The petite woman is armed with as much discretionary income as every other woman in America—she just has fewer outlets in which to spend it.

CONSIGNMENT RESALE CLOTHING STORE

High Net Profit Before Taxes:	$55,000
Average Net Profit Before Taxes:	$28,000
Minimum Start-up:	$7,500
Average Start-up:	$17,000

Open any woman's closet and you'll find perfectly good clothes that aren't being worn. Some have been outgrown; others are now too big. Some are ill-chosen gifts, while still others are the wrong color, style, cut, or fabric. Whatever the reason, most women have dozens of garments that aren't being touched—and yet, they have nothing to wear.

If only those clothes could find their way back into circulation. Thanks to a healthy resale clothing industry, they are doing just that. Resale boutiques are more than a sensible shopping alternative. They also offer an inexpensive inroad to the fashion business.

Here's why: Resale boutiques operate on consignment. Instead of going out and buying inventory, resalers take in goods from clients. When a client's item is sold, the resaler splits the purchase price with the client. In other words, your up-front investment in inventory is virtually nil. You pay for nothing until a sale is made.

Fashion First

Resale boutiques started out as outlets for cheap everyday apparel. But today, many resale shops focus on fashion. One California store we investigated sells only designer clothing, furs, and accessories. While prices are not dirt-cheap (many items sell for $100 or more), they are considerably cheaper than retail.

Quality fashions for large women is the focus at another consignment store we found. According to the store's owners, large women represent an especially promising market, since most resale shops don't carry large clothing. Large women tend to change sizes often (due to weight fluctuations), so they are eager both to buy and to sell. Other bright ideas: consignment children's, teens', and petite clothing.

Having some background in retail helps, but many consignment boutique owners are newcomers to the industry. You need a flair for display and marketing, a knack for dealing with people (especially negotiation), and an eye for fashion. If you're sharp, you can join the ranks of resale clothing entrepreneurs who are pulling in well over $100,000 annually and netting $55,000 or more.

═══════════════ BRIGHT IDEA ═══════════════

NO ORDER TOO TALL

Where does a seven-foot-tall man who weighs 300 pounds go to buy clothes? Jerry Krug hopes he'll visit one of Krug's three retail operations, Krug's Big and Tall menswear shops, in Bergenfield, New Jersey.

In 1955, Krug transformed his men's clothing store into a large-size clothing shop when he discovered that his brothers, both over six feet tall, couldn't wear anything he sold. "I realized there must be a market out there for oversized clothing," he recalls.

For years, the oversized man has suffered through bulging buttons, short pants, and collars that choke. Krug insists that he can fit almost any oversized man with stylish attire, and large men are willing to pay high prices for Krug's menswear, which brings in about $4 million a year.

"There's lots of room for growth in this industry," says Krug. That's why he has decided to embark on a franchise program, which he hopes will take Krug's Big and Tall menswear stores nationwide.

OPTICAL SHOP

High Net Profit Before Taxes:	$118,000
Average Net Profit Before Taxes:	$65,000
Minimum Start-up:	$27,000
Average Start-up:	$50,000

For decades, people have considered corrective eyewear a necessary expense. That's why the optical industry is an $8-billion-a-year business in the U.S. About 58 percent of the population wears some form of corrective eyewear. And as the population ages, that percentage is bound to increase.

But the recent boom in optical shops has as much to do with fashion as it does with ophthalmology. People are still buying glasses to see, but they're also buying glasses to look good. The old "Get a pair of black or brown" advice of yesteryear is outmoded. Today, people buy glasses to match their clothing, lifestyles, and moods. Glasses have become a consumer item and retailers are reaping the rewards.

In the past few years, America has experienced an explosion in optical shops, particularly with large chains and franchises. Typically located in malls and other high-traffic locations, these stores have brought new levels of marketing and merchandising to the eyecare industry. Consequently, the face of the business is changing, and innovative operators who can adapt to the new climate stand to make clear profits.

Emphasis on Retail

The big word in optical shops today is "retail." Twenty years ago, showing customers a few racks of frames in a dimly lit back room may have been good enough, but today optical shops are more sophisticated.

"We hired a lighting specialist. Then we had the store professionally laid out, and a graphic artist redesigned the interior," says one successful optical shop owner. "We need to look modern. Eyeglasses have become a fashion item now, not just a medical aid. It's really helped. A large chain moved in down the street, but I've still managed to increase my volume 17 percent a year. Those shops that don't adapt—I don't think they will survive."

The increased competition from chain stores and franchises may have forced independents to update their tactics, but because of their high volume requirements (a result of high overhead and discount-pricing structure), they also have neglected one vital element—quality service. That's one area in which the smaller, entrepreneurial ventures are besting the multiunit operations. Although fashion and merchandising are important to today's optical shop, finding a shop that's health- and service-oriented is also a priority for consumers.

A Matter of Degrees

There are three general levels of expertise and training in the eyecare industry. Ophthalmologists represent the highest level: They are M.D.'s who handle the most specialized and serious eyecare problems. While they can and do prescribe corrective lenses, they are also able to prescribe medications and perform surgery.

The next level of expertise is that of the optometrist. These professionals are licensed to examine eyes and prescribe corrective lenses. Many own their own optical shops or are employed by others on either a permanent or as-needed basis. In fact, many of the chains and franchises utilize their services. Some station an optometrist in the back, rent space to him or her, or have the individual come in a few times a week on a freelance basis. This way, referrals work both ways—to and from the optical shop.

Right behind the optometrist in terms of training is the optician. These individuals are experts in fitting glasses and contact lenses, and can provide patients with exactly what they want and need according to the prescription from the ophthalmologist or optometrist. Most states require that a licensed optician be present on the premises of an optical shop.

Ideally, the owner of an optical shop will also be an optician. In this way, precious start-up capital does not have to be spent on an optician's salary. But if that's not possible, this expertise can always be hired.

Sell, Sell, Sell

As we mentioned before, the best way for a small shop to distinguish itself in this business is through personalized service. At most multiunit operations, customers deal with salespeople, not opticians, with an emphasis on self-service.

"The customer ends up picking out the frames [himself or herself] at discount [outlet] or one of the other less-expensive stores," says one optical shop owner. "At a full-service shop, we'll sit down with the patient to analyze his or her features and appearance in conjunction with the lens requirements in order to recommend certain lens features when appropriate that will help the glasses cosmetically and functionally."

That's what sets the smaller shops apart and gets them referrals from independent prescribing physicians or optometrists. These stores stress quality of service as well as product. And now, for the first time, they are combining this expertise with modern retailing concepts and techniques. The result? Increased sales and strong customer loyalty.

Setting Up Shop

Years ago, the best location for an optical shop was in or near a medical building. This is no longer the case. Optical shops are thinking in terms of retail, and locating themselves accordingly.

Chains and franchises usually locate in malls, but independents have found that strip centers are better for their purposes. Mall rents are high—especially for a business that doesn't rely on impulse purchases. Moreover, mall hours may be restricted, thereby limiting the way you do business. A visible, convenient location is all you need; for most, a mall address is an expensive extra.

Locating in a mall may not increase your business, but locating near a referring source will. Having a shop next door to a referring optometrist or ophthalmologist is an excellent way to build a solid customer foundation (assuming that the optometrist or ophthalmologist will refer customers to you). It is not, however, a substitute for convenience. Look for a location that can offer you both referrals and walk-ins. If you can't find a good location near an established referral source, consider renting space in your facility to an optometrist.

Professional and Versatile

Starting a retail optical shop is not an easy proposition. The retail optical business is becoming more and more competitive. To succeed in today's market, you'll need a solid understanding of both the professional and merchandising aspects of this business. However, entrepreneurs who can combine these two elements effectively stand a good chance of prospering, even in the face of large and well-funded competition.

========== BRIGHT IDEA ==========

HOUSE CALLS ONLY

Clients don't come to Cheryl Shuman's optical shop: The shop goes out to the clients. Shuman's Los Angeles-based venture, Personal Eyes Optique, makes house calls to some 5,000 clients, including several Hollywood luminaries.

Shuman's service is the ultimate in personal attention. The process begins with a visit, during which Shuman determines the face shape, coloring, lifestyle, and personality of the client. With these criteria in mind, Shuman returns to her lab to select 500 to 600 frames that she thinks her client might like. Of these, the client may like about seventy-five, and will probably buy three or four—adding up to a per-visit average of about $950. At four or five visits a day, Shuman grosses about what a full-service shop would, but with less overhead, higher profits, and more gratification.

A quick look at Shuman's service reveals why customers have her booked for weeks in advance. Not only is she more convenient than the average optical shop, but she offers comparable prices. Because her overhead is low, she doesn't have to mark frames up exorbitantly. Better still, she hand-selects only the most fashionable, highest-quality frames, collected on regular trips to Europe and around the U.S.

All this service adds up to impressive sales at Personal Eyes—sales that Shuman believes will continue to grow. Consumers are now finally learning to love their glasses, and opticians like Shuman are partly to thank. Shuman herself is passionate in her convictions: "When I see people wearing plain old tortoise-shell glasses," she says, "I want to take them off."

KIOSK AND CART RETAILING

High Net Profit Before Taxes:	$100,000
Average Net Profit Before Taxes:	$56,000
Minimum Start-up:	$13,000
Average Start-up:	$33,000

What's smaller than the average shop, but just as well-located? At malls around the country, the answer is kiosks and carts. For a fraction of what it might cost to set up your own specialty store, you can run a kiosk or vending cart at a busy shopping center. Overhead is low, profits are high, and mall developers love the idea. "The kiosk location within a mall is space that otherwise would not be generating any income," says one developer. Recruiting these colorful businesses helps malls bring in more revenue—and adds variety for the consumer. Best of all, you can get into this business with little more than $13,000 and a good idea.

What Sells

Of course, not every product or retailer is suited to a kiosk or cart operation. Most kiosks average a fairly diminutive size of 12 feet by 12 feet, while carts are even smaller, averaging 3 feet by 6 feet. You could not, for example, fit a wide selection of big-screen TVs onto a cart.

But you could display a fair number of handmade crafts, sweatshirts, T-shirts, earrings, novelty gifts, baseball cards, software programs, fast-food items, or cosmetics from a cart. You could also peddle services like hot-tub installation or kitchen remodeling. Kiosks and carts are excellent outlets for seasonal items like Christmas ornaments, Easter baskets, or holiday gift-wrapping. Malls seem to be open to just about any profitable suggestion, as long as you aren't directly competitive with mall shops and are in keeping with mall standards (no thrift-store items, for example).

Ins and Outs of Leasing

Leasing a kiosk or cart space is both easier and more complex than leasing a regular store. It is easier because it usually involves less money and therefore less risk. It is more complex because it involves a number of variables—temporary leases vs. permanent, rental rates, and equipment requirements. These vary from developer to developer, so each transaction must be examined carefully.

The good news is that these variables make this business far more flexible than most mall operations. You may have the option of trying a business out for a month or two before committing to a long-term lease. If the developer has restrictions on the types of carts you can use, he may provide carts, saving you the expense of buying your own. You have the opportunity to shop around for the deal that best suits your needs—and that's a privilege many retailers don't enjoy.

Kiosk and cart businesses represent an excellent opportunity to try out retail ideas at a reduced risk. But don't make that your cue to take the business lightly. We have seen all kinds of businesses thrive as kiosk and cart operations, but not without the same hard work and planning that goes into any new venture.

GIVE THEM A SPIN

T-shirts continue to be a staple of the American wardrobe, thanks to their versatility. In the sixties, we tie-dyed them. In the seventies, we emblazoned smart-alecky slogans across them. The eighties saw a return to "classics," plain shirts with no gimmicks. Now, just in time for the nineties, T-shirt retailers are giving their goods a new spin—spin art, that is.

At spin-art shops, T-shirts and sweatshirts are placed on a rotating wheel and splattered with paint. At many shops, customers make their own creations. The result is glitzy, artsy, and just plain fun.

Picasso's, in the suburbs of Chicago, is one of some 250 spin-art stores nationwide whirling with activity. The store's 1988 revenues of $250,000 encouraged owners Janice Knight and Carla Coyle to expand after just nine months in business. Knight says, "Consumers love it—after the first time, they keep coming back."

CHRISTMAS ORNAMENT STORE

High Net Profit Before Taxes:	$46,000
Average Net Profit Before Taxes:	$14,000
Minimum Start-up:	$12,000
Average Start-up:	$17,000

How would you like to work three months out of the year, then take the rest of the year off? Or put in some extra effort around the holidays and beef up your annual income by $10,000 or more?

Entrepreneurs around the country are doing just that by opening their own Christmas ornament stores. Christmas comes but once a year, and most consumers can't help but go overboard—especially where ornaments are concerned. In upscale malls and shopping districts around the country, shoppers are snapping up crystal ornaments, specialty lights, and handmade decorations by the dozens.

Scout the Competition

Of course, specialty shops aren't the only places that sell Christmas ornaments. Department stores, discount and drugstores, even lawn-and-garden centers usually stock seasonal items. To maximize your chances of success, look for a location that isn't too close to the competition.

You can further distance yourself from the competition with distinctive merchandise. Focus on handmade ornaments, unusual trinkets, and other upscale items that the competition isn't likely to have. Play up the atmosphere as well. Imaginative displays, seasonal music, perhaps even complimentary hot cider, can add up to increased traffic— and increased sales.

An ideal location for a Christmas ornament store is a small shopping center, tourist area, or shopping district with heavy foot traffic. You do not need a large shop: 500 to 800 square feet is adequate, though larger shops certainly exist. One smart operator we spoke with rented an empty gas station for $300 a month his first year. Another option is renting space from a Christmas tree lot. You can get the names of previous years' Christmas tree lot operators from your city business-license office.

===============BRIGHT IDEA===============

EXERCISE WEAR

America is shaping up! From biking to weight training, aerobics to walking, people are doing more kinds of exercise than ever before—and they want to look good while they're doing it. That's why shops selling exercise wear are pulling in healthy profits.

Though exercise wear is sold at most department stores and sporting goods shops, selections there are usually slim. Specialty shops that offer a wide range of styles, colors, and sizes have a definite edge on the standard competition.

"Everyone wants a unique look, so we carry lines from as many different bodywear manufacturers as possible," says Bud Cowan, owner of Busy Body Leotard/Tights in Costa

Mesa, California. "We sell a selection of bodywear for exercise, dance, and gymnastics."

But other sports may prove equally deserving of their own shops. For instance, the recent walking craze has spawned a new breed of fitness shop specializing in walking shoes, clothing, and accessories.

EARRING SHOP

High Net Profit Before Taxes:	$57,000-plus
Average Net Profit Before Taxes:	$39,000
Minimum Start-up:	$17,000
Average Start-up:	$28,000

Earrings are the single most popular fashion accessory today. They account for over half a billion dollars in retail sales annually. True, earrings aren't exactly in short supply—department stores and boutiques of every stripe sell them—but retailers with imagination and flair can make this specialty business work.

High Profits, Hard Work

Because competition is everywhere, starting a successful earring shop requires a little homework. To make yourself stand out, you'll need an unusual collection of merchandise. "You have to travel all over looking for merchandise at the beginning," explains one successful earring retailer. "It is a very intensive business if you do it right. There are over 1,000 suppliers to choose from, and the market is constantly changing."

On the upside, however, earrings do sell. Markup is usually 100 percent, so the potential profits are good. If you're a shrewd buyer, you may be able to locate manufacturer's closeouts for less than $1 a pair—and resell them for $3 or more.

From Casual to Elegant

Earring shops vary in size, style, and location. The most upscale (and also the most lucrative) operations are mall shops that stress fashionable costume jewelry. Many cater to the teen and young adult markets with trendy, inexpensive goods. If a mall store is too rich for your blood, consider a kiosk or cart setup. You'll cut down on your inventory and lease costs and still enjoy the benefits of mall traffic. Kiosks or carts also work well at tourist attractions and other heavily trafficked locations.

Want to try your hand for a small investment? You can sell earrings on a part-time basis through swap meets. Booth space and basic merchandise can cost as little as $200, and can bring in enough per-day profits to make your weekends worthwhile.

BEAUTY SUPPLY RETAIL STORE

High Net Profit Before Taxes:	$123,000
Average Net Profit Before Taxes:	$86,000
Minimum Start-up:	$35,900
Average Start-up:	$49,600

Beauty supply stores started out as wholesale outlets for salons and mom-and-pop drugstores. But today, this is very much a retail industry. Beauty supplies account for a whopping $13 billion in sales each year—and beauty supply stores are responsible for a healthy portion of those sales.

Savvier Than Supermarkets

The shampoos, conditioners, and styling aids sold in beauty supply stores are the same ones sold in supermarkets, right? Not exactly. While beauty products are sold in supermarkets and drugstores in every community, these stores usually do not carry the most exclusive salon brands.

Who cares? Consumers do. Beauty products have come a long way in the past few decades—especially on the high end. Luxury shampoos don't just clean hair: They moisturize and "volumize." Expensive conditioners contain herbal extracts and exotic oils, while the range of available styling mousses, gels, spritzes, and sprays can force hair into shapes heretofore unknown by man. Add to this a wide variety of professional hair coloring, permanent waves, brushes and combs, ethnic hair-care products, and any assortment of cosmetics, and you have an inventory that no drugstore or grocery store can match.

Beauty supply stores have another advantage: service. The wide range of products makes good service a necessity. Yet, in most drugstores and department stores, knowledgeable service is a rarity. Many beauty supply stores hire licensed beauticians to supply product knowledge and advice. They also encourage sampling of cosmetics and fragrances—a luxury consumers don't always get in larger stores.

Emphasize Selection

Selection is the heart of the beauty supply business, so set aside a large chunk of your start-up capital for inventory. Investing $30,000 or more in beginning inventory is not uncommon, and will go a long way toward bringing the customers in—and bringing them back.

Stock as many brand names as possible. The more exclusive the brand, the better. Some manufacturers sell their products to salons only. Try anyway. If you can convince them to let you carry their products, your business will be that much more attractive to shoppers. Also consider generic and private-label products. These usually don't carry the prestige of salon brands, but their low prices and high quality appeal to many consumers.

7

SPORTS AND ENTERTAINMENT

==BRIGHT IDEA==

YOUR LIFE ON TAPE

Is your life the stuff that movies are made of? If not, would you settle for a 20- to 25-minute video? Bob Pomerantz, founder of Your Life Productions in Toronto, can put your life story on tape. Pomerantz LifeStory video productions incorporate nostalgia, comedy, and a few sentimental moments into memorable gifts for retirees, birthday celebrants, and other lucky gift-getters.

A former newspaper editor, Pomerantz quit his job in 1987 to become a full-time video producer. Before he begins making a video, Pomerantz does extensive research on the honoree's life. He hires freelance cameramen to film the videos for him, and hires former television actors or reporters to host the segments. The production involves a television crew who visits eight or nine locations to film, and the whole process, from researching to filming, takes approximately two months to complete.

"The videos are a surprise within a surprise at an unexpected retirement or birthday party," says Pomerantz, adding that the videos take an audience "from laughing to crying and back to laughing again."

SPORTS BAR

The eighties may ultimately be remembered as the decade where Americans stayed home to watch movies and went out to watch television. And in the nineties this paradoxical trend shows no sign of slowing, as sports bars continue to climb in popularity.

No one is keeping a close count, but bars and restaurants with sports motifs number more than 300 nationally, with combined sales of $2.5 billion each year. Naturally, some sports bar owners are wondering when the well is going to run dry. But will it? Considering the fervor with which America embraces the religion of sports, the time for decline may never arrive.

Let's face it, sports sanctuaries do draw an unexpected number—and unexpected mix—of worshipers. After all, sports may be the common denominator of American life, uniting computer operators, CEOs, housewives, and transit workers. People may be divided by politics, religion, and work, but sports brings them together.

As the cost (and hassle) of going to sporting events continues to rise, more and more fans are opting for a visit to the local sports bar, where good seats, good food, instant replays, and plenty of enthusiastic company are always on hand.

That's the Ticket

The costs of starting up a sports bar are as impressive as the profits. Most would-be bar owners spend $1 million to $1.5 million, depending on how many extras they include. Memorabilia, sound systems, electronic scoreboards, video games, basketball cages, simulated boxing rings, satellite dishes—they all jack up the price. It is possible to open for less than $1 million, but forgoing high-tech equipment and a friendly ambience may also diminish the appeal.

Most sports bar owners find that creative promotional

stunts are the key to attracting patrons. For example, when Chicago Cubs sportscaster Harry Carey was seriously ill several years ago, Stephen Greer, owner of She-nanigans Irish Pub & Sports Bar and the Ultimate Sports Bar & Grill, bought the world's largest get-well card. Customers at both establishments signed the six-foot greeting—ultimately totaling thousands of fans (read "paying customers"). Hosting parties for team members and auctioning off celebrity memorabilia are just a few other ways that sports bar owners grab attention.

It's a Hit

Owners say the forecast for sports bars. is bright and sunny. After all, Americans spent billions of dollars on sports-related products and services last year, and there seems to be no end in sight. As the poet William Carlos Williams wrote, "At the ballpark, the crowd rises as one." At sports taverns across America, the patrons roar as one—and that means a good time for all.

=============== BRIGHT IDEA ===============

FITNESS TO GO

"When I started my company in 1985, my friends thought I was crazy," says Cindy Pankiw, owner of To Your Health in Ontario, Canada. "They said, 'No one in their right mind is going to pay for fitness!'"

Of course, they were wrong. Not only is fitness one of the hottest industries around today, but Pankiw's particular personal training concept is a hit. Currently, she serves about fifty regular clients. "I typically go to my clients' homes two to three times a week at $40 per visit," she says.

According to Pankiw, To Your Health clients fall into four basic categories. "The first group is comprised of extremely overweight or underweight people for whom I design entire fitness and eating plans," she explains. "People in the second category are a bit overweight and would normally go to a health club, but they want someone to motivate them. This category also includes middle-aged women who have never exercised before and are self-conscious about going to a gym. The third segment consists of fairly disciplined people who don't need constant supervision, but need a program designed for them. The fourth group is made up of handicapped people."

Most of Pankiw's business comes from word of mouth. "I've found that advertising isn't really necessary anymore because the majority of my business comes from referrals," she says. How effective are those referrals? Pankiw sees ten clients a day, often stretching her work day to fifteen hours. Even for a fitness buff, that's a real workout.

VIDEOCASSETTE RENTAL STORE

High Net Profit Before Taxes:	$103,800
Average Net Profit Before Taxes:	$61,728
Minimum Start-up:	$73,150
Average Start-up:	$126,775

In the video rental business, there is good news and bad news. The good news is that videocassettes are here to stay. Today, 64 million American homes are equipped with VCRs, up from only 1.3 million in 1981, according to *American Video Network News*. And renting videocassettes has become as commonplace as buying groceries. In 1983, Americans rented 380 million videocassettes; in 1989, they rented an estimated 3.2 billion videos, according to Paul Kagan Associates, a Carmel, California, media research firm.

However, in spite of booming sales and rentals, the video industry has raced through its infancy and come face-to-face with midlife crisis. The giants of the videocassette rental industry are trying to corner the market, while many of the mom-and-pop shops are searching for new competitive edges.

The videocassette rental business still represents a tremendous opportunity for aspiring entrepreneurs with solid business sense. The days of making a mint in this business with just a little savvy are over. Enter the era of smart marketing, management, and service. Yes, you can still prosper in this business—but not without a plan.

Superstores and More

Bellflower, California, entrepreneur John English has been in the videocassette rental business since 1980. When he first started Multivideo, his was the only video store on the block. "Now there are sixty-six stores within a three-mile radius of our store," he says, "and sixty of them are independents."

It's not the sixty independents that make the biggest splash, however. The other six operations are superstores, giant locations with huge inventories and aggressive national advertising campaigns. "One small store closed its doors as soon as the [superstore's] sign went up across the street," English reports. "And another one across the street lowered its prices to 94 cents per rental to compete, but by doing so, they entered the realm of nonprofitability. The owner had to take a second job to pay the rent."

But according to English, superstores are not invincible. He argues that lowering prices is not the answer. "You have to outservice the big guys," he says. "Know your customers by name and make it more fun to be in your store. The [superstores] of the world aren't going to go away, so you have to make a bigger niche for yourself."

What's Missing

Beating the big boys at their own game can be rough going for small operators, so many find a specialty niche. When Cleburne, Texas, entrepreneur Michael Grozier stepped into his local video store to rent the latest releases, he often left the store empty-handed because eager renters had already snatched up the best movies. Disappointed, Grozier thought that there ought to be a video store that specialized in new releases.

So in 1986, Grozier opened Vidtron, his own "Top 40" video rental drive-thru kiosk featuring 175 new releases right across the street from that other video store. His theory was that people would go into the other video store, and when they came out without the video they wanted, they would give his drive-thru rental a try.

Apparently, the idea was good. Today, Grozier's original location boasts 400 new releases, and he is franchising Vidtron across the nation. Like thousands of other independent video shop owners, he has discovered that specialization is the key to survival in a highly competitive industry.

Isn't That Special?

In today's video market, more and more independents are realizing that special services or sidelines are the only way to go. Like English, small operators are trying anything they can think of to make their stores stand out. They're handing out free popcorn, stocking hard-to-find titles, offering drive-thru service, and more.

Take Patricia Polinger and Cathy Tauber, for instance. Their Santa Monica, California, store, Vidiots, specializes in hard-to-find videos. "We wanted to start our own shop, but the industry was already saturated," says Polinger. "It was far removed from the days when all you had to do was put a few videos on the shelf and open the doors. However, we did think that we could succeed with a specialty shop."

Polinger and Tauber started Vidiots in 1985 with about 800 tapes, most of them foreign films. Immediately, customers who had been looking for favorite foreign movies like *Black Orpheus* and *Picnic at Hanging Rock* flooded into the store to sign up for lifetime memberships. Today, Vidiots boasts about 5,000 members and stocks about 5,000 foreign films, documentaries, avant-garde art tapes, and movies by independent filmmakers. Polinger and Tauber don't worry much about competition from superstores: Even the most extensive of the bunch don't carry the selection that they do.

A New Bedside Manner

Specialties come in all shapes and sizes. One innovative Texas entrepreneur has taken video rentals to an untapped market: hospitals. "It's the ultimate in captive audiences," says Bedside Video's owner, Louis Karp. When Karp first introduced the idea to a local hospital, he met with some skeptics, but before long, he won them over. Last year, he opened his first successful VCR and video-rental shop at St. David's hospital in Austin, Texas.

Located next to the hospital's gift shop, Bedside Video stocks between 600 and 800 movies per store. The $6.99 rental fee includes a remote-control VCR and two movies. Bedside Video leaves cards announcing its service in each hospital room and delivers movie catalogs to interested patients. Once a patient decides on a film, a Bedside staffer delivers the VCR and the videocassettes to the room. And since everything is operated by remote control, recovering patients don't even have to leave their beds.

Karp recently opened his fourth Bedside Video location in El Paso, Texas, and is adding Nintendo and camcorder rentals (for the obstetrics patients) to his list of services. According to Karp, Bedside Video presents a "win-win-win" situation: He benefits, the patients benefit, and the hospitals benefit because he gives them a percentage of the company's gross revenues.

Picture the Future

In the rapidly changing video industry, the independents who are keeping one step ahead of the crowd have a definite edge over traditional mom-and-pop operations. While thousands of video store owners have already realized this and started adding new services, many others have ignored the competition and expect to keep plodding along with their small selection of videos. But experts agree that these shops will be the first to go should a shakeout occur.

As the video industry races into maturity, independents who want to make it to the finish line need to develop a specialty, promote their stores aggressively, and keep on top of customer preferences. Although the competition in this industry is stiff, there is still room for those who know their markets and are willing to go the extra mile to service them.

=================== BRIGHT IDEA ===================

CAMERA FOR A DAY

What's better than a day at Disney World? How about one that comes complete with a video memento? Walt Disney World in Florida began renting out video cameras in June 1988, and another rental shop has been added in Disney's Epcot Center. The park rents out an average of twenty to twenty-five cameras a day, charging a $400 deposit and $40 per day, plus $10.95 per tape.

But don't think you have to own your own amusement park to get in on this concept. Roger Thomas, president of Rent-a-Cam Inc., opened a video camera rental store near Walt Disney World in 1985 and has since added one store near Disneyland in Anaheim, California, and one in England. Thomas's Orlando store rents out about forty to fifty cameras a day. Advertising in hotel rooms accounts for a lot of business from tourists, he says, along with the fact that Rent-a-Cam charges reasonable rates—$29 the first day for an 8mm camcorder or a VHS camera. Thomas sells regular tapes for $6.95 and high-grade tapes for $9.95. His stores also rent out underwater video cameras, Sony video Walkmans, video recorder super VHS cameras, Kodak video projectors, and related equipment.

For families that can't afford their own camcorders, these services are a welcome alternative. Thomas notes that they're also useful for anyone shopping for a camera. By renting equipment, he or she can try out various makes and models before making a purchase.

SUNTANNING CENTER

High Net Profit Before Taxes:	$61,000
Average Net Profit Before Taxes:	$40,000
Minimum Start-up:	$30,000
Average Start-up:	$47,000

While the price of just about everything continues to climb, the sun gives its light for free. So why would anyone in his right mind pay money to get a tan?

For one thing, the sun doesn't always shine. Avowed tan fans use indoor tanning to maintain their golden glows all winter long. Even during the summer, people who can't reach the beach during prime tanning hours may visit a tanning salon on their off-hours. Vacationers may want to establish a base tan before taking off for a tropical climate, thereby avoiding a painful sunburn on their first days out in the blazing sun.

People are also growing wary of the sun. Medical evidence shows that sitting in the sun, soaking up ultraviolet rays all afternoon is not good for the skin. Indoor tanning salons offer a more controlled alternative to traditional sunbathing—and they're more convenient to boot.

Foul Weather's Past

Suntanning salons are a relatively new phenomenon. Though sun lamps have been sold and used for decades in this country, the concept of the commercial tanning parlor didn't take off in the U.S. until the late 1970s.

Early tanning salons were primitive. They used lamps that radiated high levels of aggressive ultraviolet B (UVB) light. To make matters worse, supervision at these salons was minimal, so customers ran a high risk of getting burned—both literally and figuratively. When safer UVA lamps were introduced, a squabble erupted between UVA and UVB manufacturers, resulting in a loss of credibility on both sides. For a time, consumers dismissed the entire business as quackery.

Now, the industry seems to be experiencing fairer weather. The most popular tanning equipment today uses bulbs that radiate higher percentages of the safer UVA light and lower percentages of the harsh UVB rays than are found in ordinary sunlight. With better equipment, more conscientious service, and an improved image, the tanning industry is back and better than ever.

Selling the Sun

All kinds of markets are receptive to indoor tanning—from Boston to L.A. The strongest regions include the Southwest, Pacific Northwest, Nevada (in hotels), the Midwest, and Mid-Atlantic states, though with the right planning and marketing, almost any metropolitan market can accommodate a tanning center.

The secret to success in the tanning business is selling annual memberships or, more profitably, packages of sessions. Monthly or quarterly packages are generally the most popular. Monthly memberships can bring in $360 or more per member per year. You can bring in additional profits by selling accessories like tanning lotion and bathing suits.

The typical tanning customer is between 18 and 45 years old, well-educated, middle- to upper-class, and interested in looking good. In some areas, like Southern California and Florida, the markets of both teenagers and senior citizens are also emerging. The ratio of male to female customers is about even, and singles outnumber married people by about 10 percent.

Although tanning doesn't provide specific health benefits, it is popular among the health-and-fitness conscious. A healthy tan is a symptom of an active lifestyle. Therefore, people who keep in shape on indoor bicycles and rowing machines are eager to complete their look with a golden tan.

A location near a health club is ideal, since you will each share some of the other's clientele. Generally speaking, look for a site with plenty of parking in a middle- or upper-middle-class neighborhood. Strip centers and freestanding store-fronts are good choices. Look for areas with plenty of upscale condo or apartment complexes; these usually house your potential clients.

Start Tanning Now

Launching an indoor tanning salon typically costs anywhere from $30,000 to $50,000 or more. In addition to the usual rent and licensing costs, the biggest expenditure you will make will be on equipment.

The average tanning operation starts out with three to

five tanning beds and about 1,000 square feet of space. At the very least, you'll need 700 to 850 square feet for a three-bed salon. The space must be divided into individual rooms, each about 7 or 8 feet high and at least 8 feet deep by 6 feet wide. Because tanning beds vary in size, you may want to select your equipment first to make sure your rooms are large enough to accommodate it.

The tanning beds themselves cost anywhere from $3,000 to $20,000 each (the average per-unit cost is $6,000). Most beds are similar in design and appearance. Variables include the size of the beds and the wattage of the bulbs (higher-wattage bulbs tan faster). Prices, maintenance packages, and warranties vary from manufacturer to manufacturer, so be sure to shop carefully. The safety and reliability of your equipment can make or break your business.

Sunny Skies Ahead

With recent reports on the effects of ultraviolet radiation, consumers are ambivalent about sitting out in the sun. Yet they're anything but undecided about having a golden, healthy tan. You can bridge the gap with a safe, well-run indoor tanning operation. Given the right combination of management and marketing, the future looks bright for this opportunity.

===================== BRIGHT IDEA =====================

ENTREPRE-NERD

The same people who shunned nerds in high school are inviting them to parties—for pay. Mike MacDonald of Berwyn, Illinois, lost his job as a computer programmer and became the nation's first entrepre-nerd. Now his company, Rent-A-Nerd® may be on the brink of franchising.

MacDonald had years of experience being a smart aleck during his school years. For Halloween in 1986, he donned a pocket protector, propeller beanie, and taped black glasses, dubbing himself the quintessential nerd. The response was so overwhelming that by January 1987 MacDonald had created a business based on the idea.

Performing what he calls "roving entertainment," MacDonald's popular alter ego, Hornby K. Fletcher, hams it up at bachelorette parties, birthday celebrations, and office parties.

Customizing his act to suit his audiences, MacDonald does Rent-A-Nerd® performances starting at $65. Performance lengths vary, but the average length is a half-hour. The business has been so successful that MacDonald sells a mail-order Nerd Diploma for $15.

=============== BRIGHT IDEA ===============

GO LEFT, YOUNG MAN

Anyone who doesn't believe it's a right-handed world isn't left-handed. From scissors to can openers, all sorts of everyday items are designed with right-handed users in mind. Now, thanks to a passel of left-handed innovators, all that may be changing. The left-handed market may be the minority, but leftys are more than willing to pay more for goods that adapt to them, not the other way around.

Just ask left-handed guitarist Tom Turrisi. Every time Turrisi wanted a new guitar, he had to have it special ordered. Guitar manufacturers didn't produce left-handed guitars unless a special request came in. Fed up with the situation, Turrisi decided to produce his own line of left-handed guitars.

"I started the Left-Hand Guitar Shop from my living room in 1972 as a mail-order operation to market new and used left-handed guitars," Turrisi says. The business grew quickly and in 1979, Turrisi changed the Springfield, Virginia, firm's name to Shane Musical Instruments.

Turrisi soon realized that the left-handed market had its limits. So he added a full line of right-handed guitars as well. Today, with healthy sales figures and distribution spanning the globe, Turrisi has made a big hit in the guitar market. He attributes much of his company's success to his hands-on management style. "I personally do 80 to 90 percent of the designs, and I walk the line at our factory to make sure of [the guitars'] quality."

AEROBIC DANCE STUDIO

High Net Profit Before Taxes:	$74,000
Average Net Profit Before Taxes:	$43,000
Minimum Start-up:	$21,000
Average Start-up:	$60,000

Fitness is here to stay—and to help ensure that fact, aerobic dance studios are recruiting new devotees all the time. Since aerobic dance first hit the big time in the 1970s, it has become a permanent part of the American exercise psyche. Aerobics bring in over $250 million in sales annually. In the words of one aerobics buff, "That's a lot of hopping around."

Flexibility Counts

Aerobic dance studios come in all shapes, sizes, and styles. Some are ultra-posh, with trendy decor and even trendier instructors. Others stress comfort and a supportive, fun environment. Large establishments keep long hours, holding classes early in the morning, throughout the day, and well into the night to accommodate busy clients. Smaller ventures hold just a few classes a day—sometimes renting space from other businesses or community centers after regular business hours.

The style and scope of your aerobics studio will depend on your goals and your access to cash. Obviously, part-time operations don't bring in as much revenue as full-scale clubs. On the other hand, your cash outlay for an hourly rental will be considerably less than it would be by the month. And as a part-timer, you could continue your regular job.

In either case, an aerobics studio doesn't require much equipment. A big, empty space and a sound system are about all you need—that is, except for talent. Qualified instructors are your most important asset in this business. Personality plays a major role in bringing people back to class. And since most aerobics studios operate on a pay-as-you-go basis, you have a definite stake in hiring instructors who draw. If you're an instructor yourself, all the better—you'll have a built-in commitment to keeping enrollments high.

===================== BRIGHT IDEA =====================

FLOWERS IN A CAN

Gardening is one of America's favorite pastimes—that is, until the actual work begins. Planning and cultivating a yard full of flowers can be a time-stealing chore. Just choosing the right plants can be a nightmare, especially if delphiniums sound like a type of marine mammal to you.

Beaverton, Oregon, entrepreneur Ruth Saltzman has the answer. Saltzman's White Swan seed collections help brown-thumbed gardeners create beautiful gardens that are "user friendly."

The seed for White Swan was planted years ago when Saltzman needed a special type of pruner that was only made in England. When she contacted the manufacturer, he suggested that Saltzman start distributing his specialty gardening products in the U.S. The company was hatched in 1978 from Saltzman's basement office.

She soon expanded into her own line of seeds, which are packaged in a shaker can and come in several selections, including the Moonlight Garden™, with a mix of plants that appear luminous at night, and Saladini®, for people who want to grow salad greens and vegetables. White Swan also manufactures bronze garden accessories. The seeds are sold through Neiman-Marcus catalogs, museums, mail order, and garden shops—"every place you can buy bubble gum," reports Saltzman.

Saltzman's knack for making things grow isn't confined to the garden; sales and profits have increased about 40 percent since she began.

=======BRIGHT IDEA=======

PUZZLING BUSINESS

Steve Richardson is the Fabergé of the puzzle trade. This master creator has been tormenting puzzle lovers for more than fifteen years with his Stave Puzzles—some of the most elaborate, difficult jigsaw puzzles in the world. False corners, pieces cut along the line of color, and odd shapes (such as people or objects) make these puzzles nearly unsolvable: just the kind of sublime torture that puzzle aficionados crave. Once fans get a taste of Richardson's puzzles, they can't wait for more.

A far cry from the normal cardboard jigsaw puzzles you find at the local drugstore, Richardson's puzzles are hand-made, wooden creations and range from $190 to $3,000 in price.

Richardson didn't plan on being in the puzzle business, but when he was laid off from his computer job nearly twenty years ago, he had to find something to support his family. He and a friend, Dave Tibbetts, started a game design company that made cardboard games and puzzles. They devised their moniker, Stave, by putting their names together. While the pair were moderately successful, it took a call from a gentleman in Boston to make the pieces fall into place.

The Bostonian asked the pair to create a wooden puzzle for his wife, and told them he was willing to pay $300 for it. "At the time we were getting $3 to $4 for our cardboard games, so we jumped at the chance," says Richardson. Since the small Norwich, Vermont, company started selling the handcrafted wonders, it has sold thousands of the puzzling creations. "We do all kinds of nasty tricks to drive puzzlers nuts," says Richardson. "And they keep coming back for more."

BOWLING CENTER

High Net Profit Before Taxes:	$500,000
Average Net Profit Before Taxes:	$110,000
Minimum Start-up:	$78,000
Average Start-up:	$250,000

It may not seem like a hip new business, but bowling represents a multibillion-dollar industry in America. In some parts of the country, interest in bowling has waned substantially over the past decade or so. But most areas still support a solid base of regular bowlers—both league members and casual bowlers. Under the right circumstances, owning a bowling alley can still be a lucrative proposition.

Buyouts Are Best

Opening a brand-new bowling center is no minor task. Costs range from $1 million to $3 million and more with no guarantee that you'll be able to drum up enough new business to break even.

Buying out an existing center is also expensive: As a rule of thumb, expect to pay at least $30,000 to $40,000 per lane, plus an additional $50,000 for refurbishing. Many prospective operators pool resources and form partnerships to finance the operation—even when a less-expensive buyout is involved. Beyond price, existing centers seem to be the better buy. You'll hit the market with an established clientele (assuming, of course, that the operation is in decent shape) and won't have to rely on an expanding market to survive. As mentioned earlier, bowling is a huge—but not necessarily growing—industry.

Finding the Right Market

As a rule of thumb, your bowling center will require a population base of 1,000 to 1,200 bowlers per lane. So if you plan to buy or build a 32-lane center, you should look for a market with at least 32,000 people.

After you look at the number of people in your area, consider the local lifestyle. In sophisticated urban areas, interest in bowling is usually in a downslide. In smaller towns and suburban areas, bowling may be as strong as ever. Again, buyers of existing centers are at an advantage: They can see firsthand how popular a place is before they invest.

In today's world, who bowls? One out of three Americans is a bowler. Of these, 9 million are league bowlers (the bowling center proprietor's strongest ally), and 60 million are casual bowlers. Of the 13 million people who consider themselves frequent (weekly) bowlers, 11 percent are under 18; 64 percent are between 18 and 49; and 25 percent are 50 or older. Interestingly, adult women represent 42 percent of the market, while adult men account for only 33 percent. About half of all bowlers have some college education (compared to 30 percent of the population at large); 33 percent have managerial or professional occupations.

As the owner of a bowling center, your success will depend largely on your ability to encourage league bowling. League bowlers mean regular business—not just on league nights, but also at practice. In deciding whether this is the right business for you, try to assess your recruiting and promotional skills. In addition to leagues, you should concentrate on bringing in recreational bowlers—families, teens, and so on. To accomplish this, aim for an atmosphere of fun and sociability—two commodities that are always in demand.

===============BRIGHT IDEA===============

PLAY-BY-PLAY PROFITS

Fred Greene has been involved with the Oakland A's in one way or another for years. As a kid he was the team's biggest fan, attending as many home games as he could, and catching the rest on the radio or television. As an adult, Greene worked at KSFO Radio, the station known as the "voice of the A's," as a production director. He was in that position in 1983, when the A's management asked for his assistance in developing a plan to improve fan participation at games.

"I borrowed my idea from the music booths where people record [themselves] singing along to their favorite songs," says Greene. "Instead of singing, my idea was to record fans announcing a real ballgame."

Greene researched the idea, found out no one else was doing it, and presented it to the management of the A's. "They loved the idea," says Greene, "but I wanted them to know how much it would cost them. I told them, 'Nothing—we'll get sponsors.'"

Greene rounded up two sponsors who agreed to pay the costs in return for an advertising jingle on each of the tapes. "After I got the sponsors," says Greene, "the A's donated the space in the stadium and agreed to pay me a percentage of the profits."

Greene's Fantasy Play-by-Play puts baseball fans in an announcer's booth and lets them call an inning of baseball while the game is actually being played. They get a choice between audio or videotape—the audio sounds like a radio broadcast; the video looks and sounds like a television broadcast. Fans are provided with all the notes and statistics, and sit in front of the microphone or camera and use the replay monitors just like real announcers. But unlike the real announcers, Fantasy Play-by-Play announcers can say and do anything they wish and nothing will be cut out.

After the inning is over, commercials and interruptions are dubbed in so that the tape sounds authentic. "We are very proud of our production work," says Greene. "People hoping to break into [sportscasting] come up here to make audition tapes."

Fantasy Play-by-Play went into business for the last three home stands of the '87 season and generated so much publicity that the A's management decided to carry it over to the next season.

The Seattle Mariners and the St. Louis Cardinals have adopted similar programs, and though Greene is sure he has a winning concept, he isn't sure that all clubs will follow his lead. "Baseball's like a big family that can't get along," he says. "If the Mets do something, the Yankees won't do it. If the A's do it, the Giants won't. And if anybody else is doing it, the Dodgers won't do it." Still, Greene believes there's room for expansion. "I'll get as many [major league teams to participate] as I can," he says.

OUTDOOR SPORTS STORE

High Net Profit Before Taxes:	$67,000
Average Net Profit Before Taxes:	$49,000
Minimum Start-up:	$130,000
Average Start-up:	$180,000

About 75 million Americans are regular participants in non-motorized outdoor activities—camping, hiking, rock climbing, canoeing, skiing, and so on. And with interest in the environment recently being rekindled, the popularity of these sports should burgeon in the years to come.

The owners of America's wilderness shops already know this. We found one well-located store grossing over $400,000 a year. Annual sales of $90,000 to $250,000 are common, and net pretax profits are typically in the 17 to 22 percent range. Ah, wilderness!

The Great Outdoors

You don't have to live in Yellowstone Park to start a successful wilderness shop. In fact, our research found Kansas City, Kansas, to be a hotbed of wilderness activity, even though the nearest wilderness is hours away in the Ozarks. To ensure a large enough market, you should operate from a population base of no fewer than 250,000 people, preferably in a community with some nearby access to mountains, forests, and streams.

Despite their frugal image, backpacking and other outdoor sports are not inexpensive. The average cost for a complete backpacking outfit is $550, including a tent, backpack, sleeping bag, outerwear, boots, and cooking utensils. Cross-country skiers spend an average of $500 to $600—and as much as $1,000 to $2,000—for skis, poles, bindings, boots, gloves, pants, parkas, caps, and gaiters. Of course, most people don't walk in and purchase all these items at once. But even bought piecemeal, they represent a healthy potential for sales.

The market for outdoor sports gear is quite upscale. Most participants are middle- to upper-middle-class with college educations and an interest in fitness. Because the market is upscale, retailers must be smart and well stocked to succeed. In addition to basic equipment and gear, offer a wide selection of accessories—knives, cooking gear, trail food, maps, and books. Also be prepared to offer information, both on your merchandise and on the activities themselves.

Some outdoor sports stores even sponsor local trips and tours. Not only does this represent an additional profit center, but it may afford you the opportunity of vacationing for a living.

============ BRIGHT IDEA ============

CLIMBING THE WALLS

Before you pack your gear and head for the Himalayas, stop: Have you done a practice climb yet?

The idea isn't as crazy as it sounds, thanks to a new trend in sports training. It's called indoor rock climbing, and it's causing a sensation in the fitness industry. The Vertical Club in Seattle, which opened in 1987, is one of just a few clubs in the country devoted exclusively to indoor rock climbing. Members don special rock-climbing shoes and scale "rocks" made of cement, plywood, or fiberglass.

According to Dan Cauthorn, co-owner of the Vertical Club, rock climbing appeals to a wide audience. "There's a percentage [of our members] who are seriously training for alpine climbing or hard sport climbing, and a percentage who are just beginning to feel their way. The bulk fall somewhere in between." Cauthorn is convinced that more indoor rock climbing gyms will be opening soon.

SPORTING GOODS STORE

High Net Profit Before Taxes:	$150,000
Average Net Profit Before Taxes:	$75,000
Minimum Start-up:	$126,000
Average Start-up:	$200,000

America's obsession with fitness has reached an all-time high. And America's sporting goods stores are feeling the growth. Sporting goods represent nearly $15 billion in annual sales—and consumers show no sign of losing interest in sports and fitness.

Fit for Shopping Only

The popularity of sporting goods isn't limited to athletes, however. The fitness boom has popularized the "active" look—sweat clothes, aerobic shoes, heavy-duty sunglasses. These and other fitness items are seen on everyone from Olympic-level athletes to kids, housewives, and beer-bellied men. And why not? Leisure wear looks good and feels good, which is more than can be said for many designer fashions.

Sales of leisure wear and other "soft goods" have shifted the focus of the sporting goods industry. Now, sporting goods stores pay as much attention to merchandising and display as they once did to stocking serious equipment. The market for real fitness gear is still going strong, but smart retailers aren't overlooking the potential in general consumer sales.

An Independent Stand

Another change that's rocked the sporting goods industry is the growth of major chains. Small operators usually can't compete with a national chain on the basis of price or advertising. Independents admit that chains have an edge in the advertising department, and many independents don't bother competing on that level. But independents are able to secure comparable buying power through buying groups.

Many independent stores give themselves a competitive edge through specialization. By focusing on one or two sports—skiing, tennis, racquetball, scuba diving, etc.—they can offer wider selection and more expert advice. Service is the one frontier yet to be claimed by most national chains.

Despite competition from the majors, independent sporting goods stores continue to prosper if they're properly run. This is no business for leisure-minded ex-jocks. Sports knowledge is a definite plus, but business sense is more important. Tight inventory control, solid management, and excellent service are critical to success in today's market.

Hard work and careful planning can pay off. Profits of $100,000 or more are not uncommon, and there is no question that America's infatuation with fitness is more than a passing fad. If you're in shape for running a dynamic, competitive, and rapidly changing business, sporting goods could be the right field for you.

================ BRIGHT IDEA ================

A STAR IS BORN

Think everyone in Los Angeles—that city of glitz and glamour—is a star? Not true. But while not everyone can become a Michael Jackson or a Cher, there is a company that's helping ordinary people live out their show-biz fantasies and become stars—if only in front of their friends and relatives.

At the Singing Store in Van Nuys, California, clients can buy "sing-along equipment"—everything from prerecorded orchestral tapes to elaborate singing machines. Co-owners Ernie Taylor and Ron Roy say their customers come from all walks of life: "We sell to band members who want the musical equipment for their gigs, and to people who just want to sing at home for enjoyment."

======= BRIGHT IDEA =======

VIDEO TO GO

What's the worst part of renting a video? Taking it back to the store, of course. That's why video delivery services are such a bright idea. Instead of schlepping to the store for the latest release, customers simply call your service and request the title they want. You deliver the tape to their home, and pick it up the following day—usually via a special lock box or other special arrangement.

The benefits of this business aren't limited to the consumer. A video delivery service doesn't need a fancy storefront or eye-catching displays. You can locate in a low-rent neighborhood and save on overhead—thereby improving your bottom line.

Starting a video delivery business isn't as simple as buying a few tapes and cranking up the family car, however. You will still need a wide selection of tapes, ample funds for marketing (remember, you won't have a storefront to attract customers), and a workable order-taking and delivery system. If you're smart enough to juggle all these variables, though, door-to-door videos could deliver just what you're looking for in a business.

8

AUTOMOTIVE BUSINESSES

CELLULAR PHONE SERVICE

High Net Profit Before Taxes:	$1,000,000
Average Net Profit Before Taxes:	$700,000
Minimum Start-up:	$70,000
Average Start-up:	$106,000

Americans spend so much time on the road these days that their cars are becoming more and more like home—or at least the office. You can't type reports or do your books in rush-hour traffic, but thanks to cellular phone service, you can call clients, set up appointments, and check in with the home office.

Technology Triumphs

Why the sudden boom in mobile phones? Cellular technology makes it possible. While the intricacies of cellular technology are beyond the scope of this book, the basics go something like this: Cellular systems depend on a dense network of radio transmitters. Each transmitter serves a "cell" a few miles in diameter. When a vehicle equipped with a cellular phone system crosses from one cell to another, automatic digital switching transfers the call from one transmitter to the next without disrupting contact.

You can imagine the range of potential uses for this kind of service. Cellular phones are a boon to busy executives. But they are also a godsend to small companies. Through cellular contact, florists, furniture stores, and errand services can keep in touch with delivery vehicles. Business owners who work at remote sites—contractors, for instance, or landscapers—don't have to be far from their phones.

Where Do You Fit In?

The cellular phone industry has many levels and categories. At the top of the industry is the operator. An operator is licensed by the FCC to provide cellular phone service to a specific geographical area. In cooperation with local government and the FCC, the operator constructs and utilizes the low-power transmitters that enable cellular communication. Competition to become an operator is horrendous. Huge sums of money and deft political maneuvering are necessary just to put yourself in the running. Though becoming a cellular operator isn't a bad opportunity per se, it is beyond the grasp of the average entrepreneur.

For most small-business owners, the primary opportunities in this industry lie in sales, installation, and service. One popular option is becoming an agent or reseller. A reseller purchases or leases a series of phone numbers from a cellular phone operator, then resells them to consumers. The customers belong to the reseller, who administers their cellular phone accounts. Agents are similar, but limit their services to sales. After collecting their commissions, they turn over all accounts to the operator for servicing.

Some resellers and/or agents also handle the installation and sales of the consumer's hardware. Clearly, this is also a lucrative business. Cellular phone units cost the end user $500 to $2,500 per unit, plus $150 to $200 for installation. If a reseller signs on 100 new customers in a year, and installs their equipment for them at an average total cost of $1,000, his or her gross on equipment alone is $100,000. As the industry ages, the market for maintenance and repair will expand substantially.

Start with Research

Obviously, the best markets for new cellular phone businesses are those in which service is relatively new. Before you get into this business, check out the potential in your local market. Are cellular phones just catching on, or are they old hat? How many agents and resellers already exist? Is there room in your market for new (or improved) services—and if so, where?

Becoming an agent can be as simple as setting up a home office, making a few contacts, and selling like mad over the phone. If you want to become a reseller, your risk and investment increase. You'll need a letter of credit for each phone number at the time you purchase it, upping your potential investment to $10,000 to $25,000 or more. Installation and maintenance services can increase your initial cash outlay to between $25,000 and $40,000, to accommodate service bays, inventory, test instruments, and facility.

=================== BRIGHT IDEA ===================

WINDOWS WHILE YOU WAIT

According to Los Angeles entrepreneur Violetta Hargitay, owner of Custom Window Tinting, people would rather see the world through glare-filtered glasses. "Even if I saw hundreds of window tinters in the Yellow Pages, I still wouldn't be concerned about losing business," she says. "The opportunities in window tinting extend as far as the eyes can see glass."

Hargitay may be overstating, but not by much. Considering the number of automobiles on the road today (not to mention the amount of glass used in architecture), the opportunities in this field are fairly vast. And Custom Window Tinting has an edge: Instead of making customers come to her, Hargitay brings the window tinting service to them. "I drive to wherever the car is parked and tint the windows on the spot," she says. "I bring all of the equipment I need with me, so the owner doesn't have to do a thing." All this for about the same price as her garage-based competitors.

Door-to-door service is a true luxury—and that's reflected in Hargitay's clientele. Her list of clients includes Sylvester Stallone, Aaron Spelling, and Madonna. "I tint their personal car windows, and I also do a lot of work right at the movie studios for production companies," she says. "I've worked on the *Dynasty* set and on movies like *Lethal Weapon* and *Midnight Run.*"

Though servicing celebrities was one of Hargitay's original goals (just her way of breaking into the movie business), she also works with plenty of ordinary folks. All told, the tinting business has this entrepreneur seeing green. "I'm always booked at least two weeks in advance," she says, "and I'm becoming so busy that I'll be hiring an assistant soon."

TIRE DEALER

High Net Profit Before Taxes:	$175,000
Average Net Profit Before Taxes:	$130,000
Minimum Start-up:	$65,000
Average Start-up:	$90,000

Tires come and tires go—and in the process, tire dealerships make a tidy profit. The Automotive Information Council reports that some $14.2 billion worth of new replacement tires are sold annually. Retreads account for an additional $1.89 billion. And the market shows no sign of slowing. As long as people drive their cars, trucks, vans, and motorcycles, the tire business will continue to thrive.

Tires for All Stripes

Just about anyone with a vehicle is a potential customer. For aspiring business owners, the most accessible market is consumers and small fleet owners. Commercial business is also an option, but competition for big accounts like Greyhound and Bekins is fierce. To start, it's best to focus on the individual consumer and small-business person (the owner of a local delivery service, the neighborhood taxi company).

What will your tire store offer that other stores don't? Your best bet is service. The first thing tire shoppers need is information. What makes one brand of tires better than another? Do they need snow tires and why? Arm yourself and your staff with knowledge, and you'll be off to a good start.

Tire stores generally offer mounting, balancing, and alignment services in addition to sales. You may also wish to offer brake service, battery sales, shock absorber installation, and a few other auxiliary services to supplement your business.

Outside of the basics, though, it's important to emphasize convenience. Look for a location that's convenient to shopping, transportation, and/or businesses. Make your hours amenable to working people—open early in the morning or on weekends, for instance, or stay open until nine or ten a few nights a week. Also consider the preferences of your local market. Will they most appreciate a clean, comfortable waiting area? Or are rock-bottom prices their primary concern?

What's in a Name?

One of the major decisions you'll face as a start-up tire retailer is whether or not to become a name-brand dealer. Major companies like Goodyear and Firestone sell their goods to anyone, but give their best deals to franchised dealers. Also, by becoming a franchised dealer, you gain the right to advertise your association with that company. And though front-end costs may be higher, you will also enjoy valuable name recognition.

Many small tire dealers do not become franchisees, however. They stay independent, buying lesser-known goods or generics and selling them at lower prices. The choice is yours: With proper management, either option can work. Check out the local competition. Are they primarily single-brand dealers or independents? Usually, the best road is the one less traveled.

Don't Forget the Smarts

The tire business is a stable one, but it isn't foolproof. In addition to the millions of skills you need to start any successful venture, you'll need to learn plenty about tires—how to sell them, how to mount them, how to maintain them. Customers will rely on you for expertise, and you had better be prepared to deliver.

To succeed, you will also need a solid marketing plan. Too many businesses fail before anyone knew they existed. Map out an aggressive marketing strategy, including direct-mail coupons, flyers, and newspaper ads. This, combined with reliable service, should put you on the road to prosperity.

===============BRIGHT IDEA===============

GETTING THE BRAKES

In today's automotive aftermarket, it seems that no service is too specialized for consumer tastes. At Brake Express, based in Irvine, California, car owners come in solely for sales, installation, repairs, and maintenance on brakes, struts, and shock absorbers.

Brake Express' business is anything but on the skids: Since the company began franchising in 1988, more than twenty Brake Express shops have opened. And this is just one example of the growing trend toward specialization in auto repair. Focusing on a single aspect of car repair enables business owners to maximize efficiency—and buying power.

At the same time, consumers seem to put their faith in specialized repairs. "If I take my car to a brake specialist," explained one happy client, "I know they know what they're doing. They aren't 'branching out' into a new area and using my car as a guinea pig. When it comes to brakes, you really don't want that."

================ BRIGHT IDEA ================

RETRO LIMO

All limousine services are not created equal. When Leonard Rivero and his wife, Maria, decided to expand their limousine service, they did it with a twist. Instead of buying another limousine for their one-car operation, the Seattle couple built their own. In 1987, Leonard, who had been building custom cars and street rods since high school, created what he calls the world's first "neoclassic" limousine, designed with lines similar to the 1932 Duesenberg.

The limousine attracted so much attention and drew so many requests in the Seattle area that the Riveros decided to move their business to Southern California, a more lucrative market for limousine services. In 1988, they opened Limodream in Huntington Beach, California, and began manufacturing more neoclassic limos. "Southern California is an excellent area for a limousine service, but it's very competitive, so you need an edge to succeed," says Leonard.

The Riveros limousines became so popular that Clenet International Ltd., a neoclassic car manufacturer in San Luis Obispo, California, offered to produce the retro limos on a larger scale in September of 1989. "Instead of building one car at a time, I can now go at full production," says Leonard, who is vice president of marketing and sales and technical advisor for Clenet, in addition to running Limodream with Maria. Three different models of Rivero's neoclassic limousines can be purchased through Clenet International.

The Riveros now have three neoclassic limos in their fleet, as well as two conventional stretch limos. Eight-passenger neoclassical limos rent for $90 an hour, about twice the standard rate for limousine service.

USED-CAR RENTAL AGENCY

High Net Profit Before Taxes:	$50,000
Average Net Profit Before Taxes:	$38,000
Minimum Start-up:	$43,000
Average Start-up:	$60,000

Sometimes you want to rent a snazzy new car—and sometimes you wouldn't mind renting a heap. For many car renters, cosmetics don't count. Any reliable transportation will do—particularly if it means saving a few dollars.

Used-car rentals are catching on in cities where regular car rentals are wildly expensive. But consumers aren't the only ones saving. Start-up costs on a used-car rental agency are substantially lower than those on a conventional agency. That makes this business more accessible to aspiring entrepreneurs.

Think Young

Who rents used cars? The largest potential market is young adults. They're interested in saving money, and may also enjoy the novelty of renting, say, a red '66 Mustang convertible. Baby boomers (who may once have owned '66 Mustang convertibles) are another strong market, as are older drivers who need occasional transportation.

Though used-car rental agencies are popping up in all types of communities, densely populated urban or suburban areas are most desirable. Look for a community of at least 250,000 people, with a minimum of 30,000 people within a three-mile radius.

In marketing your business, keep your eye on the youth market. College campuses and young urban apartment complexes are good targets. Also establish contact with local travel agencies and tourist offices. Flyers are a reliable method of spreading the word. Coupons are even better, since they stress the economy angle of your business.

The Rental Business

Perhaps the most complicated part of starting a used-car rental agency is setting up the right procedures. When you rent out a car, you entrust a major piece of equipment to a virtual stranger. Screen your customers carefully, and get your payment up front in cash or on credit cards (no checks).

Have an attorney help you write a rental contract that covers all your bases. For instance, stipulate that the car must be returned at the agreed-upon time, and that overdue vehicles will be reported stolen within 24 hours unless you're contacted. Make sure your contract (and your insurance policy) covers you in the event of an accident or theft.

The size and style of your fleet will depend on your plans—and your pocketbook. You do not need hundreds of cars to start, but don't cut corners too closely. You should have enough cars to send out with a few spares in case one of your rentals breaks down. An added marketing point: Offer 24-hour emergency service within a reasonable radius of your agency. This kind of backup will help convince skeptical consumers to try your service.

=================== BRIGHT IDEA ===================

HELP GRANTED

Buying a new car can be a frustrating experience for the novice. That's why John Longenecker, Jr., a former sales and finance manager for auto dealerships, started his Long Beach, California-based company, The Auto Advantage. The home-based company helps new-car buyers in twenty-one states purchase their cars.

"I launched The Auto Advantage while I was working for another auto dealership," says Longenecker. "Two elderly sisters came to the dealership looking for an automobile, but didn't buy one from me. However, they called a week later and asked if I would assist them in buying a car at another dealership. It was an unusual request, but I did it because I knew they needed help. Soon I began helping friends buy cars, and The Auto Advantage evolved."

For his services as an independent buying agent, Longenecker charges $195. For this fee, he will investigate the maximum discount on the vehicle of the customer's choice. "I provide clients with a detailed report," says Longenecker, "and I'll arrange everything related to the sale—right down to the appointment date for delivery."

AUTO PARTS STORE

High Net Profit Before Taxes:	$100,000
Average Net Profit Before Taxes:	$73,000
Minimum Start-up:	$54,000
Average Start-up:	$88,000

It's no secret that car repairs and maintenance cost a bundle. Yet many routine jobs are simple to do. With the right tools and supplies, mechanically inclined car owners can save themselves hundreds of dollars annually on labor. Beyond repairs and maintenance, car owners spend billions annually on auto-related accessories—from automatic radio antennas to car covers, glare-cutting devices, and exterior striping.

Sales like these make the retail auto parts business a growing industry in the U.S. Entrepreneurs with merchandising ability are taking the industry by storm, opening multiple locations and bringing in gross sales of $250,000 to $500,000 once established.

The Changing Market

Once upon a time, auto parts stores were side-street operations, complete with greasy salespeople and girlie pin-ups. These operations still exist, but the newest breed of auto parts retailer is slicker. Clean, well-lighted stores have attractive displays and friendly salespeople—and many customers are women (so forget the girlie pin-ups).

Domestic auto parts were once the sole stock. Today, most auto parts dealers carry import parts as well. The import market is simply too large to overlook. And let's face it, foreign cars break down, too.

Another change in the industry is the focus on location. While you don't need a fancy mall location to start an auto parts business, you don't necessarily want a deserted warehouse, either. Suburban shopping areas are a good choice, since most of your customers will be young married men and women.

THE TRUCK STOPS HERE

These days, when people climb into the family car, chances are good it's a light truck or van. Light trucks are not only replacing the family station wagon, but they're also a hit among business owners who need practical, durable transportation.

Light trucks, vans, and jeeps have become so popular, in fact, that they are giving birth to their own field of automotive specialty. Rick Pewe's shop, the Republic Off-Road Center in Tempe, Arizona, draws off-road truck owners from all over the state to buy hard-to-find parts and to service their trucks and jeeps. An uncommon expertise in jeeps, old and new, has allowed Pewe to run a successful mail-order business as well. Pewe's five employees mail the parts to individuals and wholesale dealers all over the U.S.

Jeff Solomon-Hess, editor of *Aftermarket Business*, says, "Although the light truck market may reach a saturation point in the mid-1990s, young families are buying the all-purpose minivans and getting accessories for them." Thus, businesses specializing in truck repair, detailing, or accessories can expect a boom in business down the road.

LET THE SUN IN

In today's commuter lifestyle, cars are more than transportation—they're practically second homes. That's why many car owners are willing to spend a little extra money to make their cars more livable.

Just ask Bob Richards, who left a sales position with a major automotive manufacturer twelve years ago to pursue then-untapped opportunities in sunroof sales. In his first year of business, selling and installing custom Toyota Celica T-top packages, Richards' company, Pacific Auto Accessories,

Inc., grossed nearly $1 million. At that point, Richards expanded his T-top market to include other domestic and foreign sports cars.

According to Richards, the 1990s will see the demand for aerodynamic styling packages and spoilers increasing. These accessories accounted for approximately 65 percent of the more than $10 million Pacific Auto Accessories grossed in 1989. And who knows what new gadgets the automotive market will introduce in the next few years? As Americans continue to spend more and more time in their cars, the market for auto amenities should continue to grow.

SELF-SERVICE GAS STATION

High Net Profit Before Taxes:	$99,600
Average Net Profit Before Taxes:	$36,000
Minimum Start-up:	$15,600
Average Start-up:	$50,000

According to the American Petroleum Institute, some 79 percent of motorists nationwide use self-serve pumps (except in New Jersey and Oregon, where self-serve stations aren't allowed). And who can blame them? Full-service stations charge as much as 35 cents extra per gallon simply for putting gas in the car. Old-fashioned full service—in which windows were wiped, fluids were checked, and tires were inspected—has gone the way of the whalebone corset.

The self-service trend began in the 1970s, when gas prices soared. To combat the rising prices, stations began offering self-serve at a discount. Now, pumping your own has become a fact of life.

It has also simplified the gasoline business. In the old days, service station owners stressed service—including repair services on which they could earn a steady income. But with the advent of self-service stations, it became obvious that repairs and gas sales were not inseparable. Eliminating the "service" element of the classic service station simplified needs for labor, equipment, and space.

Finding a Station

Start your investigation by calling oil companies in your area—both major companies and small ones. Their representatives can provide solid insights into your local market and offer leads on vacant properties for sale or lease. Also check the "business opportunities" and "commercial properties for rent" columns in the classified sections of your local papers.

Before you decide on a particular location, ask as many people as possible for information. You want to know which neighborhoods show potential, which suppliers are reliable, which pitfalls can be avoided. If you buy or lease an existing station, show the books to an accountant experienced in evaluating service-station operations before you sign.

Check out opportunities with major oil companies, but don't rule out starting an independent station. Working with smaller suppliers may save you money on gas and monthly rent. On the other hand, the name-recognition and credit associated with a national brand may translate into increased sales. Again, information is your best resource. Ask each supplier about the relative benefits of his service, then make an educated decision.

The best way to evaluate a station's potential is to spend some time at the station before you buy or begin leasing. This way, you can learn the day-to-day operations and see firsthand how much business is done.

================ BRIGHT IDEA ================

AUTO ART

From the moment he first stepped into a toy car as a child, Jacques Vaucher has loved automobiles. In 1981, Vaucher turned that infatuation into a business, creating the world's first automotive art gallery. The New York City gallery, l'art et l'automobile gallery ltd., on 34th Street, houses his world renowned and highly acclaimed collection of "automobilia."

The gallery is filled with everything from antique car models and paintings to books and posters. It attracts auto aficionados from all over the world, and brings in annual sales of $2 million.

Granted, this isn't a business that can survive on every street corner. But according to Vaucher, you don't have to be a born aesthete to make the business work. He broke into the art world almost by accident. "I organized a successful show for a German artist at the U.S. Grand Prix at Watkins Glen, New York," he recalls. Once on the fast track, Vaucher couldn't get off.

============================= BRIGHT IDEA =============================

MOTORCYCLE MANIA

Are you mad for motorcycles? You aren't alone. Motorcycles enjoy a cult following that shows no sign of slowing down. If you're a motorcycle junkie, why not turn your hobby into a business?

While you don't have to be a motorcycle fanatic to sell bikes, a genuine interest in cycles really helps. Garry Robertson was a motorcycle enthusiast long before he opened Robertson's Power & Sports, a retail motorcycle and snowmobile shop in Sanford, Maine. He learned the ins and outs of the business while working for a sporting goods store. When the chance to open his own shop came along, Robertson jumped.

Since Robertson took over the shop, his sales are nearly double those of his predecessor. He believes his affection for the merchandise makes the difference. "My love of motorcycling—and snowmobiling—really helps me in my business," he says. "When I'm dealing with my customers, they can sense that I know what I'm talking about, so they listen to me and trust my recommendations."

===================== BRIGHT IDEA =====================

VEHICLE LEASING

With the price of new cars going through the roof, more and more people are opting to lease their new vehicles instead of buying. What was once considered beneficial only to fleet owners, large corporations, and high-mileage drivers is now being sought by individual consumers. In the last decade, the number of cars leased to individuals has tripled—and is expected to continue multiplying in the years to come.

Getting started in the leasing business isn't as difficult as you might think. You can break into the leasing business on a limited basis by becoming a lease broker. As a broker, you simply match clients with the vehicles they want, then sell the transaction to a bank or finance company. Once the lender buys the transaction, your liability ends and your profit is made. To become a broker, you need little more than a working phone, business cards and stationery, a business license, and a transportation consultant's license. You can work from your home to start.

Once you're established—or if you're especially ambitious to start—you can expand your services and become a leasing company. A leasing company provides the same services as a brokerage, only instead of selling the final transaction, the leasing company retains the title to the property and collects lease payments from the lessees. Though running a leasing company entails considerably more work, it also offers a higher profit potential. You may also enjoy increased credibility with banks and lessees if you're a full-blown company instead of a broker.

Ultimately, the size and scope of your company will depend on your level of commitment and expertise. To learn more about vehicle leasing, contact the National Vehicle Leasing Association in Los Angeles. Or consider working for an established leasing company.

9

OUT OF THE ORDINARY

OUTRAGEOUS FASHION

Breaking into the fashion business isn't easy, so it helps if you have a gimmick. Though current fashion trends make outrageousness an ever more elusive goal, at least one fashion maven managed to make a splash. For Los Angeles entrepreneur Kari Vander Schuit, bustiers were her entrée into fashion manufacturing.

When Vander Schuit was a little girl, her mother warned her, "Always wear nice underwear in case you're in an accident." Vander Schuit went one better. In 1985, with a $500 loan, she designed a line of custom bustiers that may not cause accidents, but certainly stop traffic. Five years later, 24-year-old Vander Schuit had parlayed this small investment into a $200,000 business bearing her name.

Bustiers—strapless bras or corselets—have supported women's bosoms for at least 100 years. Now they're being worn by stars like Madonna, Victoria Principal, and Barbara Carrera.

Before launching her own company, Vander Schuit attended Los Angeles' Fashion Institute and worked in a fash-

ion showroom at the California Mart. She made her first
bustier as a costume to wear while singing backup at a local
nightclub—and was swamped with compliments. After a
year of performing, she dove into design full-time. "I started
in my dad's dark, dusty cellar with a light and two sawhorses
topped with an old door for a desk," she recalls.

Vander Schuit would wear the bustiers into trendy boutiques, carrying a shopping bag stuffed with samples. Three
out of five store buyers wanted them. Then, about two years
ago, Vander Schuit laid out her samples for a top manufacturer's representative and was instantly signed. Almost immediately, she received $20,000 worth of orders from
clothing stores in California.

To accommodate an increase in business (there are more
than 100 accounts to date), Vander Schuit designs from
home, then contracts out the piecework. Her bustiers sell for
$180 to $350 in upscale outlets in Beverly Hills, Melrose
Avenue, and around the world. Several department store
chains have also expressed an interest.

Now Vander Schuit is diversifying. She has developed a
range of separates, such as matador pants, lace and chiffon
bolero jackets, and gossamer chiffon skirts. Next on her
crowded agenda: marketing her fashions to catalogs, cruise
ship gift shops, and the bridal industry.

========================= BRIGHT IDEA =========================

ONLY THE LONELY

This cruel, cruel world is no place for the lonely. Yet millions
of Americans live alone, be they single, divorced, or widowed.
Lucky for them, some innovative businesses have come up
with a slew of products and services to keep these lonely
individuals company.

Traditional solutions to the loneliness problem include
dating services, senior day care, and travel agencies that
specialize in singles' tours. Moreover, pet stores, bookstores,
video rental companies, and all-night croissant parlors see

their share of lonely people. But what's new for the alone and lonely? In today's market, the answer is "plenty."

For the scared and lonely, Provo, Utah-based Gregory (Mannequin) Inc. has come out with Gregory, a fiberglass passenger-seat and home companion useful for scaring off highway assailants, burglars, and other evildoers. The brainchild of company founder Stephen Bennett, the mannequin is available through mail order only. But Gregory is no cheap date; without clothing, he sells for a cool $295.

For the bored and lonely, Ken Winans' World Famous Electric Toilet Co. in Binghamton, New York, has put a man in a toilet. Winans' electric toilet is attached to a power pack; when it is turned on, the lid lifts up and a dummy's head pops up and peers over the rim of the toilet seat. First introduced to the market in April 1988, the man in the toilet comes in an on-off model that sells for $600, and a remote-control model that sells for $875.

Finally, for the loud and lonely, Takara, a Tokyo-based firm, has introduced Rock 'n Flowers. Created by Isamu Katoka, these funky flowers shake, rattle, and roll to the hip sounds of today's cool tunes. The secret: Inside each of these little hipsters is a tiny microchip that senses sound and vibration and prompts the blossoms to move and groove in response to the music. Distributed by Waco Products Corp. in Fairfield, New Jersey, Rock 'n Flowers retail for about $29.95.

===================== BRIGHT IDEA =====================

PICTURE THIS

Do you love to surf but hate getting your hair wet? California entrepreneurs Peter Schworer, Mike Thornton, and Rick Ireton have just the thing for you. For $5, they will instantly snap your photo framed in the curl of a pounding eleven-foot-high wave—and nary a drop will muss your curls.

Of course, it's only make-believe. Surf Foto's Giant Wave is a spectacular 3-D replica of the Banzai Pipeline in Oahu,

Hawaii. Unveiled for the Fourth of July weekend in 1988, the prototype wave is made entirely of glass, wood, metal, and foam. Sixteen feet long and 7 feet wide, the 1,500-pound prop is amazingly realistic. The main feature is a real surfboard mounted "in the tube" and layered with ten coats of clear fiberglass. Sturdy enough to hold an entire basketball team, the surfboard is mounted on a steel frame and supports up to 1,000 pounds.

"It all started about two years ago," says co-owner Schworer. "We were lifelong surfers. One day we had our picture taken with a Ronald Reagan cardboard cutout, and, being surfers, we figured there had to be something better than this. After a few beers at a local bar, we developed the concept of the Giant Wave. We built the prototype ourselves, through three months of trial and error."

Wherever Surf Foto goes, enthusiastic crowds are quick to line up. "The response has been overwhelming," says Thornton. "We've been all over Southern California at county fairs, street fairs, grand openings, and special events like fund-raisers at schools and churches." Schworer snapped over 300 pictures in six hours at the Hometown Street Fair in Manhattan Beach, California. At $5 per posed picture, that's over $1,500 gross sales in a single day.

But manning events isn't the only way these partners are making money. They've started manufacturing fiberglass waves so that other entrepreneurs can follow in their footsteps. Several amusement parks have expressed an interest in the concept, and one suntan-lotion manufacturer may use the wave in a promotional tour.

Meanwhile, waves aren't the only option for photo-minded entrepreneurs. In addition to the Ronald Reagan cutouts that inspired Schworer and company, there are operations that let customers dress up in antique clothing, pose for fake covers of their favorite magazines, get dolled up for glamour shots, and even pose in their favorite lingerie. If you can picture it, almost anything goes.

=== BRIGHT IDEA ===

WEATHER, ANYONE?

Before the tarp is rolled up and "Play ball" echoes through the stadium in Kansas City, groundskeeper George Toma calls Sara Croke for a little inside information. Since 1986, meteorologist Croke has been predicting rain, tornadoes, snow, and sunny skies for the Kansas City Royals, as well as for a host of businesses.

After three years as a television meteorologist, Croke decided to put her forecasting talents to use on a private basis and started Weather Or Not in Kansas City, Missouri, in 1986. Her first client, the Kansas City International Airport, hired her to alert them in case of ice or snowfall—hours before that first flake ever hit the earth. "We can call at three A.M. to say that it's going to start snowing at five A.M. and that there will be an inch of snow on the ground by six A.M.," explains Croke.

Thirty-one-year-old Croke, who promises to "babysit storms while you sleep," also keeps a watchful eye on the skies for the Kansas City Chiefs, the Kansas City Track Club, and the Kansas City International Raceway, as well as for numerous construction and production companies.

Why do these people pay for what most of us think should be free information? Well, Croke does much more than simply predict rain. She claims she can pinpoint when rainstorms will start and stop—almost to the minute—and also predict which neighborhoods will be hit hardest.

This kind of information can save construction and production companies thousands of dollars in lost time. For instance, when New Moon Production Services shot the "Nike Bo and Bo" commercial featuring Los Angeles Raider and Kansas City Royal Bo Jackson and guitarist Bo Diddley, they called Croke to get the latest word on the weather in Kansas City. Thanks to Croke's forecast, they were able to schedule a one-day shoot.

Saving other companies money has turned into a profitable venture for Croke, who has taken Kansas City by storm.

That meteorologist predicts that Weather Or Not's revenues could reach as high as $75,000 this year.

NOTHING TO SNEEZE AT

If you think money doesn't grow on trees, John Sneed can prove you wrong. Sneed, a Missouri entrepreneur, has made a business of collecting allergy-causing pollen from trees, grasses, flowers, and weeds. With his two sons, he harvests the weeds and pollens on his farm, and sells them to pharmaceutical companies for use in making allergy medications.

Using a ten-foot-wide vacuum cleaner that sucks up the pollen, Sneed harvests weeds from March 1 through October 1. Before it is sold, the pollen is refined in his plant until it is 99.5 percent pure, meeting Food and Drug Administration standards.

Sneed, a former farmer, says he "just happened to be at the right place at the right time" when he got his start in the pollen-harvesting business. In 1963, he worked for a pollen-harvesting company and became interested in the business. In 1970, the Sneeds began harvesting their own weeds under the name Ashland Farm Botanicals. "The weed-harvesting business doesn't have the ups and downs of farming because weeds grow regardless of the weather," Sneed reports.

Pharmaceutical firms pay from 40 cents to $80 or $90 a gram for weeds and pollen, Sneed says, depending on how prolific a weed is and how much allergy it causes.

FISHING FOR GOLD

Fishing for a lucrative business? Consider starting a goldfish farm. Today, goldfish come in all shapes and sizes. Fancy fantails with lion heads, special coloring, and telescopic eyes bring in top dollar—retailing for $12 and more. Then there are koi, special Japanese carp that come in a rainbow of colors. At the bottom of the social register are feeders, standard nickel-and-dime fish that are used primarily to feed other, more exotic fish.

Whatever the breed, goldfish represent a major market here in the U.S. One goldfish farm, Hunting Creek Fisheries, Inc. in Thurmont, Maryland, raises and sells millions of goldfish each year. Hunting Creek Fisheries occupies some 125 acres of land with 110 different ponds.

Hunting Creek owner Ernest Tresselt joined the family business in 1950 and immediately started looking for ways to improve farming methods. He began by developing the right fish food. "We have worked with [Zeigler Brothers] for twenty or twenty-five years to produce healthy, fast-growing, colorful fish," says Tresselt. Keeping ponds aerated (full of oxygen), safe from predators (including osprey and herons), and free of disease have presented additional challenges. Tresselt's philosophy has been to stay one step ahead of potential problems. As a result, Hunting Creek has been a perennial success in a relatively competitive business.

Hunting Creek Fisheries sells to wholesalers, distributors, and a few select retailers in the U.S., Canada, and Europe. Judging from Tresselt's success, the key to this business is keeping abreast of industry advancements and staying in touch with the market. "We produce fish to meet the demand of each market," including pet stores, aquarium pools, and "feeders," says Tresselt. "Each of these markets wants a particular type of fish. The biggest demand quantity-wise is from the feeders' market, which uses small fish as food for larger fish."

=========================== BRIGHT IDEA ===========================

FIRST AID FIRST

First aid is a lot of things—lifesaving, critical, important— but it usually isn't convenient. That is, except when entre-

preneurs Jan Turnbull and Nadine Miller, cofounders of
F.A.S.T.—First Aid Supplies and Training Limited—in Sur-
rey, British Columbia, are involved. F.A.S.T. makes custom-
designed first-aid kits for retail and industrial use.

Turnbull and Miller started F.A.S.T. after meeting at a
Christmas party. At the time, Turnbull was operating a CPR
(cardiopulmonary resuscitation) training company with another partner, and Miller was working as a district coordi-
nator for the Canadian Cancer Society. Tired of teaching
classes, Turnbull wanted to expand her business to sell a
first-aid kit she had developed that was packaged in a soft,
waterproof bag which she figured made it easy to carry yet
hard to damage. Miller, whose job had given her a strong
business background, was actively searching for a venture to
start.

Miller bought out Turnbull's former partner, and F.A.S.T
was born. For the past two years, the partners have been
busy promoting the customized first-aid kits, which range
from $14.99 for the basic "Ouch Pouch" to $3,000 for a
complete trauma kit.

"We have more than twenty different kits," says Turnbull.
"Clients tell us what they want and we design the kits to
meet their specifications." That includes packaging as well
as the first-aid supplies.

The first-aid kits have attracted high-end retailers like
Abercrombie & Fitch as well as the British Columbia Ministry of Forests. The partners sell their kits to retail stores,
government agencies, and construction companies, as well
as marketing the kits at recreation shows.

========================= BRIGHT IDEA =========================

FLYING HIGH

San Diego businessman Don Tabor gives new meaning to the
expression "Go fly a kite." The innovative entrepreneur took
a favorite hobby—kite flying and design—and turned it into
a lucrative kite-making business called Top of the Line Kites.

The business Tabor and his wife Pat founded in 1982

developed during a lull in Tabor's former yacht restoration business. To occupy his time until the boat business picked up, Tabor bought a single-string kite and starting flying it. Dissatisfied with the kite's lack of speed and maneuverability, he began to make some modifications.

As soon as the alterations were complete on his unique two-string, delta-shaped kite, Tabor knew he was onto something. "Whenever I flew my experimental kites, crowds would gather around to watch," he says. And with good reason: The new five-foot kite surprised onlookers by performing precise in-flight maneuvers.

"People would always come up to me with awed expressions on their faces," he says. Before long, they were coming up to him with money in their hands. Tabor sold his kites for $120 to $220 apiece, and within six months of designing his first kite, he was making more money selling kites on the weekend than restoring yachts during the week. To protect his invention and officially launch his business, he patented his kite and began searching for distributors. However, the business initially hit turbulent winds. "At first, the response was fairly negative." Tabor says. "Distributors couldn't see a customer paying $150 or more for a kite."

By taking a different approach—going directly to potential customers at kite competitions and festivals—the Tabors eventually met with success and made the business a full-time venture. "We sold our mobile home, bought an industrial sewing machine and materials, and rented a commercial space," says Tabor. In the first year, the couple grossed $15,000, and by the second year, sales increased to $45,000. After another year of what Tabor calls the "grass roots" approach to sales, the company's sales were up to $150,000, and they're still soaring today.

What happened to those skeptical distributors, you ask? Today, they're singing a different tune. One kite dealer told Tabor, "We couldn't believe you would try to sell a kite like that. We just laughed our tails off. Now I need a dozen!"

BUILD A BETTER DIAPER

To most of us, the best diaper is no diaper.

Unfortunately, however, diapers are a fact of life. Even in our technological age, diapers remain a primitive item—but perhaps not for long. Entrepreneurs around the country are devising new improvements on the basic diaper.

The trouble with diapers (beyond the obvious) is that they're a hassle. Pinning on a regular cloth diaper requires the dexterity of a surgeon, while more convenient disposables pose a threat to the environment. One company has responded by introducing a disposable diaper that is biodegradable, thereby easing the consciences of pollution-conscious parents.

Ghassem and Linda Nikkhoo of Pasadena, California, starting manufacturing their own pinless cloth diapers in 1988. Tired of pinning his child into loose-fitting cloth diapers, Ghassem, an engineer with the Los Angeles fire department, decided to design his own. Made of cloth with Velcro straps, Nikkhoo's pinless diapers were a hit. "People who saw them on our son Daniel asked where they could get a set," says Linda.

In 1988, the couple formed DM Enterprises and began marketing the diapers from their home by mail order, under the name Bun E. Wraps. The diapers rapidly grew in popularity, attracting a marketing company, Communication Arts Corp., in April 1989.

"They changed the diaper's name to Baby Bottums, and our company's name to DM Naturalwear," says Linda. "We now distribute Baby Bottums nationwide through diaper-service newspapers. Sales have doubled every year."

========== BRIGHT IDEA ==========

A SHADY BUSINESS

Americans have found a new fascination with old things—
old cars, old songs, old paintings, and even old lampshades.
Linda Panek, owner of the Antique Lampshade Co. in Mis-
sion Viejo, California, has found her niche creating replicas
of antique lampshades.

All of Panek's lampshades are designed after Victorian era
lampshades, and are handmade. She adds to their authenticity by using old tablecloths and curtains she gathers from
garage sales and secondhand stores.

Panek began making lampshades as a hobby from her
home in 1983. She taught herself the technique while living
in Portland, Oregon. She says that creating these
lampshades is an art, one that took her a while to master. "I
spent a lot of time wrapping wire," says Panek, "and I've
thrown away [many] lampshades in the process."

But Panek's perseverance and practice paid off. She heard
that The Old Spaghetti Factory, a restaurant chain in Southern California, needed lampshades for their restaurants,
called them, and got an interview with the vice president. "I
took them samples of my work, and they loved them," says
Panek. "It was my first big sale."

Along with her corporate accounts, Panek sells to retail
stores and to homeowners directly. In addition, Panek adver-
tises in lighting magazines, which brings in calls from retailers. Being an entrepreneur means being flexible, so
Panek has not limited herself to making lampshades. She
also sells replicas of antique lamps and repairs antique
lampshades.

===== BRIGHT IDEA =====

STEALING THE SCENE

Like many photography companies, Christopher Norris' business meant continually contending with the unpredictable actions of Mother Nature. "When it rained the day before a shoot, the whole wedding party still had to clomp through the mud to find the perfect spot," the Cleveland-based photographer laughs. "And we had to endure the steamy heat of the summer, too, in order to get just the right picture."

So Norris took nature into his own hands and developed the first outdoor studio—right in his own backyard. "It took us a full year of work to conceive and develop, but today, we have five acres of perfect scenery right behind our indoor portrait studio," he says. "We have a lake with a waterfall, beautiful gardens, a bridge, and gazebo—even a swing set."

Brick walkways join one scene to another, eliminating problems like dirtied shoes and muddied gowns. "The response to the outdoor studio has been even better than we expected," says Norris. "Our business has doubled."

===== BRIGHT IDEA =====

PERRIER FOR PUPS

He steals the steak off your dinner plate. He laps up leftovers of duck-liver pâté. But Fido just won't touch the Perrier. What will his friends think?

Help is on the way. At F.J.'s Blackhawk Supermarket in Danville, California, dogs can drink their own brand of bottled water. And in fact, Thirsty Pup water doesn't just sell—it sells out.

"Thirsty Pup is merely distilled water, just like the water that people drink," says Michael Angelo, vice president of the supermarket. "The only difference is that it's labeled for dogs. Their owners seem to love it."

Apparently, F.J.'s customers don't hesitate to treat their animals to the same luxuries they enjoy. Says Angelo, "We introduced Thirsty Pup as a novelty item last summer, but it sold out the first day and we've received hundreds of calls since then." The company plans to distribute the product to other stores in Southern California and then branch out to the East Coast.

===BRIGHT IDEA===

LONG ON SHORTS

If you think underwear should be plain and white, you're part of a dying breed. Today, underwear is getting nearly as much attention as the fashions that go over it—and that goes for men as well as for women.

Just ask Nicholas Graham, the president and CEO of San Francisco-based Joe Boxer Corp. "We design novelty underwear and men's loungewear, among other things," reports Graham, who started the company in 1985. "The underwear uses graphic humor that's often on the cutting edge."

What he means is, Joe Boxer underwear is likely to feature polka dots, cartoon bananas, or dogs chasing their tails. Once, Graham designed "Joe Entrepreneur" underwear patterned with $500 bills. The Secret Service showed up on his doorstep and confiscated every pair (you're not allowed to print U. S. money on merchandise). In addition to underwear, Joe Boxer manufactures knitwear, swimwear, activewear, and sportswear, with annual growth of 200 percent.

But let's face it, shorts are where it's at. Just ten years ago, men hardly looked beyond basic briefs. Now, wild colors, witty designs, and luxurious fabrics (silk, pinpoint oxford cloth, cotton sateen) are getting a closer look. And for entrepreneurs, the underwear market could be a good entrée to the competitive world of men's fashion. After all, what's on the surface doesn't count: It's what's underneath.

=========== BRIGHT IDEA ===========

WATER ON WHEELS

If you can't sell them, rent them. So figured Dale Norton-Schock, president of August Moon Spas in Bloomfield Hills, Michigan. Norton-Schock is the brain behind the Traveling Tub, a small redwood and cedar house, pulled by a 25-foot trailer, which contains an eight-person Jacuzzi. The hot tub is surrounded by benches, so as many as a dozen revelers can wait their turn—even in the middle of a Michigan snowstorm.

The Traveling Tub was originally conceived to promote Norton-Schock's spa-products company. But Norton-Schock discovered that he could recoup expenses by renting out the tub for $125 on weeknights, $199 on weekend nights, or $275 for a weekend. He simply backs the trailer into a client's driveway, grabs a garden hose, and fills the 375-gallon spa. The trailer has a heater, pump, bubbler, and lighting system.

Approaching 100 rentals per year, Norton-Schock thinks his distributors and licensees, who buy tub units for $25,000, will soon put Traveling Tubs on the map. Meanwhile, Norton-Schock is comfortable putting other people up to their necks in hot water.

=========== BRIGHT IDEA ===========

GIVE THEM A RING

Old phones never die, they just become collector's items. Antique telephones of all shapes and sizes are the newest decoration craze in homes and offices—and this is good news to Elliott Tuckel, who started Antique Telephones Ltd. in Stamford, Connecticut, in 1987.

"I went to an antique telephone show one day and bought my first two-box Western Electric telephone, hung it in the family room, and fell in love with it," Tuckel recalls. "From then on, I got as much information as I could on old phones, joined a trade association, and met all kinds of collectors."

But Tuckel sells more than just vintage phones. A former executive at TIE Communications, a major manufacturer of electronic digital phone equipment, he has struck a balance between restored antique telephones and refurbished secondhand telephone systems. He realized that many antique phone collectors are interested in modern telephone systems as well. "The two lines work well together," says Tuckel.

To accommodate both old and new telecommunications products, the company has two divisions—Antique Telephones Ltd. and ATL Enterprises.

Tuckel estimates his annual sales at $500,000. "I could never have achieved [such success] with just the antique telephones," says Tuckel, who plans to expand his products to include phone equipment from AT&T, Toshiba, and Iwatsu.

165 Guides to Help You
Start Your Own Business

ANIMAL-ORIENTED BUSINESSES

Business Guide No. ....Reg. Price/Sub. Disc.

1033. Pet Hotel & Grooming Service $69.50/59.50

1007. Pet Shop $69.50/59.50

APPAREL BUSINESSES

Business Guide No. ....Reg. Price/Sub. Disc.

1161. Children's Clothing Store $69.50/59.50

1272. Large-Size Women's Apparel Store $29.50

1152. Lingerie Shop $69.50/59.50

1290. ``Sweats''-Only Retailing $69.50/59.50

1043. T-Shirt Shop $69.50/59.50

1229. Used/Consigned Clothing.............$69.50/59.50

1333. Women's Accessories Store $69.50/59.50

1107. Women's Apparel Shop $69.50/59.50

AUTOMOTIVE BUSINESSES

Business Guide No. ....Reg. Price/Sub. Disc.

1076. Car Wash $69.50/59.50

1268. Cellular Phone Service $69.50/59.50

1146. Detailing, Automobile ....$69.50/59.50 †

1224. Limousine Service $69.50/59.50

1054. Oil-Change, 10-Minute $69.50/59.50

1197. Parts Store, Auto $69.50/59.50

1018. Sales, Consignment $29.50

1108. Used-Car Rental Agency $69.50/59.50

2330. Used Car Sales ....$69.50/59.50 ‡

2329. Vehicle Leasing ....$69.50/59.50 ‡

What's inside an Entrepreneur
How-to Business Guide:

Imagine having a group of business owners unselfishly confide the details of their success in the kind of business you want to start. They reveal profits and operating costs. They share their solutions to typical problems. They give you their own secrets for making the business "hum"

That's what it's like inside an Entrepreneur Business Guide. You get inside information compiled, analyzed and categorized by our staff and put in a form that's easy to read and understand. It gives you the equivalent knowledge of many years of experience in your new business even though you're just starting out.

Each Guide is approx. 200 pages in length, and comes full tabbed for easy reference in its own handsome, vinyl-covered loose leaf binder.

YOU LEARN–

■ The profit potential for this business ■ The specific start-up costs ■ The size and scope of the market ■ How many hours a week it will take ■ How to easily manage this type of business ■ Site selection and lease negotiation ■ What kind of equipment you may need ■ Anticipated sales volume ■ Sample floor layout of your operation ■ How and where to buy supplies ■ How to set prices ■ How to set up an accounting system ■ Licenses and permits you may need and where to get them ■ How to hire and set up payroll when you're ready ■ How to advertise and promote your type of business.

Each guide comes with an unconditional 90-day money back guarantee (from date of purchase, less shipping and handling).

CALL TOLL FREE 1-(800) 421-2300
in California 1-(800) 352-7449

COMPUTER-ORIENTED BUSINESSES

Business Guide No. ....Reg. Price/Sub. Disc.

2335.	Bookkeeping Service	$69.50/59.50
1221.	Consulting & Temporary-Help Service,	$69.50/59.50
1288.	Desktop Publishing	$69.50/59.50
2333.	Diet & Meal Planning	$69.50/59.50
1084.	Hardware Store, Computer	$69.50/59.50
1265.	Home Computer, Making Money With a	$69.50/59.50
1237.	Information Broker	$69.50/59.50
1256.	Repair Service, Computer	$69.50/59.50
1253.	Software Locator Service	$69.50/59.50
1261.	Software Store	$69.50/59.50
2332.	Tax Preparation Service	$69.50/59.50

CRAFT & MANUFACTURING BUSINESSES

Business Guide No. ....Reg. Price/Sub. Disc.

1304.	Craft Businesses	$64.50/54.50
1262.	PVC Furniture Mfg	$64.50/54.50

EMPLOYMENT SERVICES

Business Guide No. ....Reg. Price/Sub. Disc.

1051.	Employment Agency	$69.50/59.50
1228.	Executive Recruiting Service	$69.50/59.50
1260.	Resume Writing & Career Counseling	$69.50/59.50
1189.	Temporary-Help Service	$69.50/59.50

FAST-FOOD BUSINESSES

Business Guide No. ....Reg. Price/Sub. Disc.

1270.	**Chicken, Flame-Broiled**	**$29.50**
1083.	Cookie Shop	$69.50/59.50
1126.	Donut Shop	$69.50/59.50
1073.	Hamburger/Hot Dog Stand	$69.50/59.50
1187.	Ice Cream Store	$69.50/59.50
1056.	**Mobile Restaurant/ Sandwich Truck**	**$29.50**
1006.	Pizzeria	$69.50/59.50
1279.	Restaurant Start-Up	$69.50/59.50
1079.	Yogurt (Frozen) Shop	$69.50/59.50

FOOD & SPIRITS, RETAIL

Business Guide No. ....Reg. Price/Sub. Disc.

1158.	Bakery	$69.50/59.50
1202.	Coffee & Tea Store	$69.50/59.50
1173.	Convenience Food Store	$69.50/59.50
1296.	Health-Food/Vitamin Store	$69.50/59.50
1024.	Liquor Store	$69.50/59.50
1295.	**Muffin Shop**	**$29.50**

HOMEBASED BUSINESSES

Business Guide No. ....Reg. Price/Sub. Disc.

1278.	Bed & Breakfast Inn	$69.50/59.50
1288.	Desktop Publishing	$69.50/59.50
1258.	Freelance Writing	$69.50/59.50
1306.	Gift Basket Service	$69.50/$59.50
1265.	Home Computer, Making Money With	$69.50/59.50
1092.	Import & Export	$69.50/59.50
1015.	Mail-Order Business	$69.50/59.50
1308.	Silk Plants	$67.50/59.50 †

HOME FURNISHINGS

Business Guide No. ....Reg. Price/Sub. Disc.

1212.	Used/Consignment Furniture Store	$69.50/59.50

PERSONAL SERVICES

Business Guide No. ....Reg. Price/Sub. Disc.

1194.	Dating Service	$69.50/59.50
1170.	Hair Salon, Family	$69.50/59.50
1264.	Image Consulting	$69.50/59.50
1274.	Nail Salon	$69.50/59.50
1239.	**Tutoring Service**	**$29.50**
1330.	Wedding Planning Service	$69.50/59.50

PHOTO-RELATED BUSINESSES

Business Guide No. ....Reg. Price/Sub. Disc.

1209.	One-Hour Photo Processing Lab	$69.50/59.50
1204.	Videotaping Service	$69.50/59.50

PUBLISHING BUSINESSES

Business Guide No. ....Reg. Price/Sub. Disc.

1067.	Newsletter Publishing	$69.50/59.50

RECREATION & ENTERTAINMENT BUSINESSES

Business Guide No. ....Reg. Price/Sub. Disc.

1242.	Balloon Delivery Service	$69.50/59.50
1186.	Bar/Tavern	$69.50/59.50
1269.	Bowling Center	$69.50/59.50
1308.	Compact Disc-Only Store	$69.50/59.50
1132.	Hobby Shop	$69.50/59.50

**CALL TOLL FREE 1-(800)421-2300
in California 1-(800)352-7449**

1342	Mobile DJ	$69.50/59.50
1124	No-Alcohol Bar	$69.50/59.50
1100	Pinball & Electronic Game Arcade	$69.50/59.50
1226	TV & Movie Production	$69.50/59.50
1192	Videocassette Rental Store	$69.50/59.50

RESTAURANTS, SIT-DOWN

Business Guide No.		Reg. Price/Sub. Disc.
1289	Diner	$69.50/59.50
1279	Restaurant Start-Up	$69.50/59.50
1156	Sandwich Shop/Deli	$69.50/59.50

RETAIL BUSINESSES, MISC.

Business Guide No.		Reg. Price/Sub. Disc.
1318	Baby Store	$69.50/59.50
1277	Beauty Supply Store	$69.50/59.50
1293	Bookstore, Children's	$69.50/59.50
1331	**Character Merchandise Store**	**$29.50**
1135	Cosmetics Shop	$69.50/59.50
3361	Buying Products From Other Countries	$59.50/49.50
1143	Flower Shop	$69.50/59.50
1144	Framing Shop, Do-It-Yourself	$69.50/59.50
1306	Gift Basket Service	$69.50/59.50 †
1218	Gift, Specialty Store	$69.50/59.50
1323	Kiosks & Cart Business Opportunities	$69.50/59.50
1222	Multilevel Marketing Sales, How to Develop	$69.50/59.50
1316	**Off-Price Retailing**	**$29.50**
1283	Party Goods/Gift Store	$69.50/59.50
1325	Print/Poster Store	$69.50/59.50
1214	Religious-Gift/Book Store	$69.50/59.50
1340	Sock Shops	$69.50/59.50
1337	Silk Plants Shop	$69.50/59.50 †
1322	Sports Memorabilia Store	$69.50/59.50
1117	Used-Book Store	$69.50/59.50
1182	Wedding Shop	$69.50/59.50

SELF-IMPROVEMENT BUSINESSES

Business Guide No.		Reg. Price/Sub. Disc.
1172	Physical-Fitness Center	$69.50/59.50
1046	Self-Improvement/Insight-Awareness Seminars	$69.50/59.50

SERVICES TO BUSINESS

Business Guide No.		Reg. Price/Sub. Disc.
1223	Advertising Agency	$69.50/59.50
1292	Advertising, Specialty	$69.50/59.50
1236	Apartment Preparation Service	$69.50/59.50
1317	Business Brokerage	$69.50/59.50
1307	Business Development Center	$69.50/59.50
1207	Collection Agency	$69.50/59.50
2328	Construction Cleanup	$69.50/59.50 ‡
1329	Construction Interior Cleaning, New	$69.50/59.50
1151	Consulting Business	$69.50/59.50
1232	Coupon Mailer Service	$69.50/59.50
1328	Freight Brokerage	$69.50/59.50
1237	Information Broker	$69.50/59.50
1336	Instant Sign Store	$69.50/59.50
1034	Janitorial Service	$69.50/59.50
1098	Liquidator Selling Distressed Merchandise	$69.50/59.50
1332	Mobile Bookkeeping Service	$69.50/59.50
1962	Money Broker	$84.50/74.50
1031	Parking Lot Striping & Maintenance Srvc	$69.50/59.50
1280	Pest Control	$69.50/59.50
1324	Public Relations Agency	$69.50/59.50
1339	Referral Services	$69.50/59.50
1136	Secretarial/Word-Processing Service	$69.50/59.50
1150	Surface Cleaning, Mobile	$69.50/59.50
1148	Telephone-Answering Service	$69.50/59.50
1157	Trucking, Cross-Country	$69.50/59.50
1012	Window-Washing Service	$69.50/59.50

SERVICES TO THE HOME

Business Guide No.		Reg. Price/Sub. Disc.
1053	Carpet-Cleaning Service	$69.50/59.50
1215	Catering Service	$69.50/59.50
1291	Closet Customizing	$69.50/59.50
1334	Home Inspection Service	$69.50/59.50
1275	**House Sitting/In-Home Care**	**$29.50**
1314	Interior Designer	$69.50/59.50
1105	Kitchen Remodeling	$69.50/59.50
1198	Lawn-Care Service	$69.50/59.50
1343	Mini-Blind Cleaning	$69.50/59.50
1160	Maid Service	$69.50/59.50
1249	Painting, House	$69.50/59.50

1285.	Pool Cleaning & Repair $69.50/59.50
1012.	Window-Washing Service $69.50/59.50

SERVICE BUSINESSES, MISC.

Business Guide No. ....Reg. Price/Sub. Disc.

1309.	Check Cashing Service $69.50/59.50
1058.	Child-Care Service $69.50/59.50
1037.	Dry-Cleaning Shop $69.50/59.50
1313.	Event Planning Service $69.50/59.50
1306.	Gift Basket Service $69.50/59.50
1298.	Instant Print/Copy Shop $69.50/59.50
1326.	**Instant Shoe Repair Shop $29.50**
1162.	Laundromat $69.50/59.50
1042.	Mini-Storage Facility $69.50/59.50
1287.	Packaging & Shipping Service $69.50/59.50
1310.	Personal Shopping Service $69.50/59.50
1341.	Pet Sitting $69.50/59.50
1320.	Private Investigator $69.50/59.50
1147.	Private Mailbox Service $69.50/59.50
1335.	Senior Day Care $69.50/59.50
1150.	Surface Cleaning, Mobile $69.50/59.50
1154.	Travel Agency $69.50/59.50
1077.	**Vinyl-Repair Service $29.50**

SPORTS BUSINESSES

Business Guide No. ....Reg. Price/Sub. Disc.

1022.	**Bicycle/Moped Shop $29.50**
1286.	Sporting-Goods Store $69.50/59.50
1322.	Sports Memorabilia Store $69.50/59.50

STREET-VENDING BUSINESSES

Business Guide No. ....Reg. Price/Sub. Disc.

3360	Sourcebook of Products for Flea Markets............................$59.50/49.50
1127.	Shrimp Peddling $64.50/54.50
1299.	Vending Businesses $69.50/59.50

MISCELLANEOUS BUSINESSES

Business Guide No. ....Reg. Price/Sub. Disc.

1091.	Burglar Alarm Sales/ Installation ...$69.50/59.50
2327.	Buying Foreclosures ....$69.50/59.50 ‡
1227.	Government Contracts, How to Obtain $69.50/59.50
1282.	Herb Farming $69.50/59.50
1222.	Multilevel Marketing Sales, How to Develop $69.50/59.50
1153.	Real Estate Company, Flat-Fee $69.50/59.50
1284.	Real Estate, Complete Investment Guide $69.50/59.50
1071.	Seminar Promoting $69.50/59.50

IMPROVING YOUR BUSINESS ABILITY

Business Guide No. ....Reg. Price/Sub. Disc.

3402.	Business Plan, Developing A $59.50/49.50
7205.	Calif. Business Start-Up $64.50/54.50
3370	Complete Government Resource Guide Complete Set $99.50/89.50
3371	Western Region......................$49.50/39.50
3372	Midwestern Region.....................$49.50/39.50
3373	Southern Region $49.50/39.50
3374	Eastern Region $49.50/39.50
1321.	Credit Consulting $69.50/59.50
7000.	Incorporation Kits for Any State (Specify State) $59.50/49.50
1327.	Lessons From America's Successful Entrepreneurs $54.50/44.50
1312.	Personal Financial Planner $84.50/74.50
1111.	Promotional Gimmicks $69.50/59.50
1999.	Complete Library of All Business Guides.................$5,450/$4,450
1315.	SBA Loan Guide $74.50/64.50
1319.	Standard Business Forms for the Entrepreneur $59.50/49.50

‡ Audio Cassettes Plus Reference Book
† Supplemental Video available

Satisfaction Guaranteed

You have nothing to lose. If you follow the instructions and they do not work for you, return the business guide within 90 days with a simple note, telling us where we went wrong. Yes, return the business guide within 90 days and we'll return the purchase price, less shipping and handling.

Place your order by mail or phone.

To order by phone:
Call TOLL FREE: 1(800)421-2300
CA residents call: 1(800)352-7449

For rush shipments:
Please call our toll free number:
6a.m.-8:30p.m. Monday-Friday
7a.m.-3p.m. Saturday Pacific Coast time.

For customer service or billing inquiries call:
1(800)345-8614
In CA call: (714)261-2325 • 8a.m.-5p.m. • Monday-Friday

To Order by phone: ☎

In order to save you time when ordering, please have the following information ready:

1. Completed order form.
2. Credit card number and expiration date.
3. Customer code number: **9N184**
4. Please note: We do not take C.O.D. orders.

To Order by Mail: ✉

1. Be sure to fill out the order form completely.
2. Please check all your entries for legibility.
3. Please include a home <u>and</u> work phone number in case we have a question about your order.
4. Be sure to include your complete street address for parcel deliveries. U.P.S. will not deliver to P.O. boxes.

**CALL TOLL FREE 1-(800)421-2300
in California 1-(800)352-7449**

ORDER FORM

Entrepreneur Business Guides

Save up to 20% on Entrepreneur Guides when you subscribe to *Entrepreneur Magazine*

Guide #	Guide Title	Price
	California Residents add 6.25% sales tax	
	Add $6.75 for shipping and handling	
	Add $2.00 shipping and handling for each additional business guide	
	Entrepreneur subscription fee	
	Canadian orders add $15.50 shipping and handling for first guide, $5.00 for each additional guide	
	Total	

Worldwide orders accepted with U.S. funds. Add $35.00 per business guide for shipping. To ensure delivery we mail air parcel post only. Prices subject to change without notice. Allow 3-4 weeks for delivery. **No C.O.D.s.**

SUBSCRIBE NOW!

To qualify for lower prices, see below for information on subscribing to *Entrepreneur Magazine*. If you are already a subscriber, write your subscription number from the label of a recent magazine here: _____

Yes! I want the subscriber discount that comes with my subscription to *Entrepreneur*. I understand I will receive a $10.00 discount on any Entrepreneur guide, **except guides priced at $29.50.** (In Canada add $10 per year. Overseas orders add $20 per year.)

Start my subscription at the basic rate checked:

⌐ 3 years (save 57% off cover price) $47.97
⌐ 2 years (save 50% off cover price) $37.97
⌐ 1 year (save 46% off cover price) $19.97

Payment by:
⌐ Check or money order enclosed

Charge my:　　　⌐ VISA　　　⌐ MasterCard　　　⌐ Discover　　　⌐ Am Exp

Credit Card #_____ Expiration Date _____

Sign Here_____ (No orders shipped without exp. date & signature)

Name _____

Address _____

City _____ State _____ Zip _____

May we have your phone # in case we have questions regarding your order?

Work Phone (____) _____ Home Phone (____) _____

Mail to:　2392 Morse Avenue • P.O. Box 19787 • Irvine, CA 92713-9438
Call toll free: 1-(800) 421-2300 • in California 1-(800) 352-7449　**9N184**

CALL TOLL FREE 1-(800) 421-2300
in California 1-(800) 352-7449